MAXIMKO
ART

SCHOOL OF MANGA:

HOW TO DRAW MANGA AND ANIME FACES FOR BEGINNERS

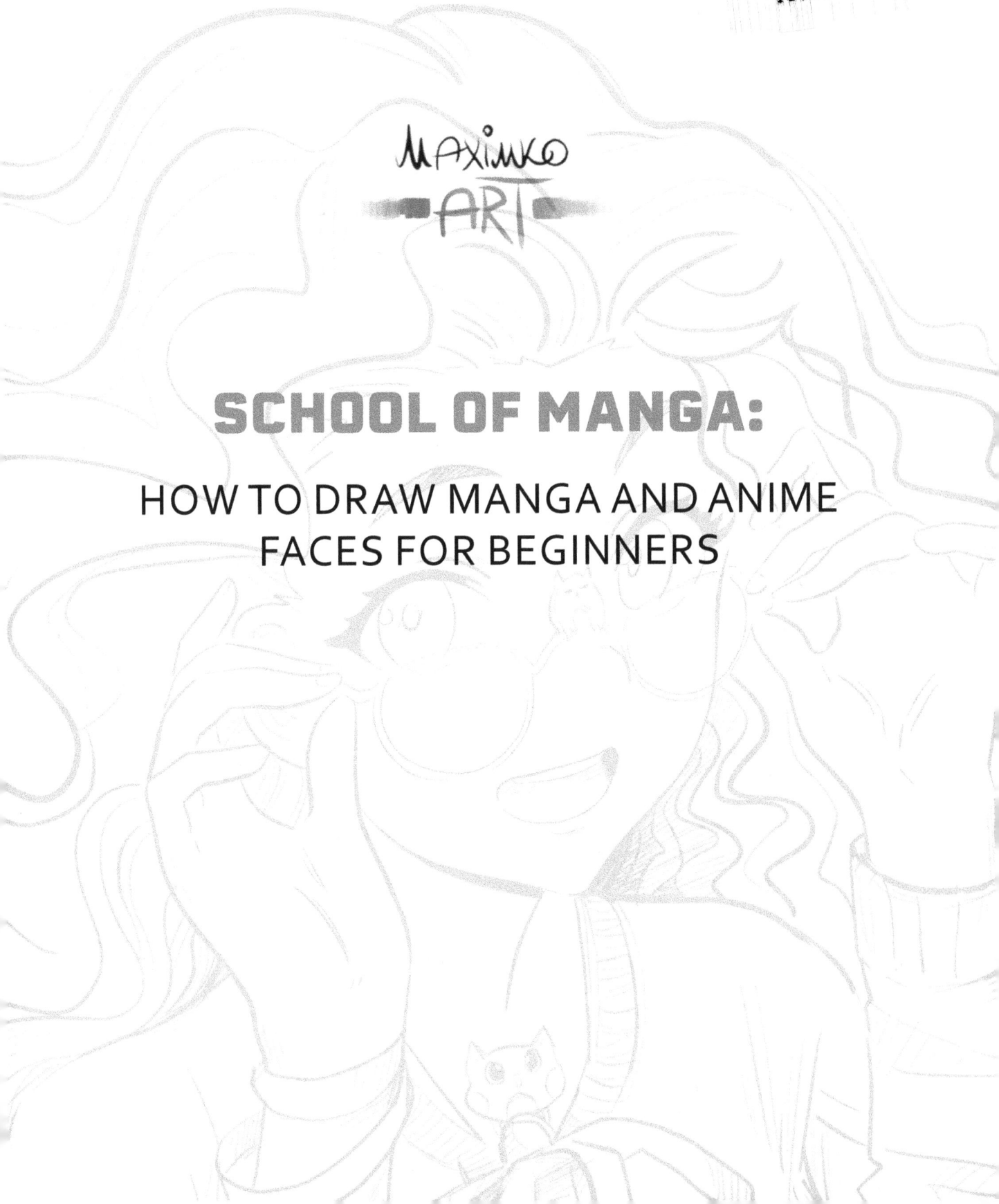

TABLE OF CONTENTS

4   **ABOUT THE AUTHOR**

6   **INTRODUCTION – TIPS FOR USING THIS BOOK**
- 8   PUMP UP YOUR CREATIVE BICEPS STEP BY STEP
- 9   STEP 1: EYES, NOSE, EARS, MOUTH AND HAIR
-      STEP 2: FACES FROM THREE STANDARD PERSPECTIVES
-      CHIBI, SHOJO/SHONEN, SEINEN/JOSEI
- 10   STEP 3: PERSPECTIVE, FACIAL EXPRESSIONS AND AGE LEVELS
-      STEP 4: HEADGEAR AND SHADING
- 11   TO CONCLUDE: DRAW A MANGA SHORT STORY
- 12   HOW IMPORTANT IS THE MANGA DRAWING STYLE?
- 13   FINDING YOUR OWN DRAWING STYLE

14   **CHAPTER 1 – DRAWING MATERIALS**
- 16   1.1 TIPS FOR DIGITAL DRAWING
- 19   1.2 TIPS FOR DRAWING WITH PENCIL AND INK
- 20   EXERCISE: CIRCLE DRAWING AND HATCHING

24   **CHAPTER 2 – HOW TO DRAW EYES, EARS, LIPS & NOSE**
- 26   2.1 DRAWING EYES STEP BY STEP
- 32   2.2 DRAWING EARS STEP BY STEP
- 36   2.3 DRAWING NOSES STEP BY STEP
- 39   2.4 DRAWING THE MOUTH STEP BY STEP

48   **CHAPTER 3 – HOW TO DRAW NECK, NAPE & HAIR**
- 50   3.1 DRAWING THE NECK, NAPE, AND SHOULDERS STEP BY STEP
- 58   3.2 DRAWING HAIR STEP BY STEP
- 66   3.3 DRAWING BEARD STEP BY STEP

70   **CHAPTER 4 – DRAWING A CHIBI BOY FROM THREE ANGLES**
- 72   4.1 CHIBI BOY: FRONT VIEW
- 76   4.2 CHIBI-BOY: SIDE VIEW
- 80   4.3 CHIBI-BOY: ¾ VIEW

84   **CHAPTER 5 – DRAWING A SHOJO GIRL DRAW FROM THREE ANGLES**
- 86   5.1 SHOJO GIRL: FRONT VIEW
- 90   5.2 SHOJO GIRL: SIDE VIEW
- 94   5.3 SHOJO GIRL: VIEW ¾

98   **CHAPTER 6 – SHONEN STEP BY STEP**
- 100   6.1 SHONEN BOY: ¾ VIEW

104 CHAPTER 7 – SEINEN MAN FROM THREE ANGLES
106   7.1 SEINEN MAN: FRONT VIEW
110   7.2 SEINEN MAN: SIDE VIEW
114   7.3 SEINEN MAN: ¾ VIEW

120 CHAPTER 8 – PERSPECTIVE DRAWING
122   8.1 PERSPECTIVE FROM ABOVE
128   8.2 PERSPECTIVE FROM BELOW

134 CHAPTER 9 – FACIAL EXPRESSIONS
136   9.1 JOY
140   9.2 SURPRISE AND FEAR
143   9.3 ANGER AND RAGE
146   9.4 GRIEF

150 CHAPTER 10 – DIFFERENT HEAD SHAPES
152   10.1 ROUND HEAD SHAPES
154   10.2 RECTANGULAR HEAD SHAPES
156   10.3 TRIANGULAR AND EGG-SHAPED HEAD SHAPES
158   10.4 OTHER HEAD SHAPES

160 CHAPTER 11 – DRAWING DIFFERENT AGING STAGES
162   11.1 DRAWING A GRANNY
166   11.2 DRAWING A GRANDPA
170   11.3 OLDER MAN (ADVANCED LEVEL)
172   11.4 BABY FROM THE FRONT
174   11.5 BABY FROM THE SIDE
176   11.6 BABY FROM A ¾ VIEW
178   11.7 AGING PROCESS: FROM BABY TO GRANDPA

184 CHAPTER 12 – HEADDRESSES UND NECK ACCESSORIES
186   12.1 HEADPHONES
188   12.2 MAGICIAN HAT
192   12.3 VIKING
196   12.4 TOP HAT
198   12.5 BASEBALL CAP
200   12.6 SPACE HELMET

204 CHAPTER 13 – COVER DRAWING STEP BY STEP
206   13 COVER DRAWING

ABOUT THE AUTHOR

Hello, I am Maxim Simonenko. I was born in Dnepropetrovsk, in Ukraine. From the age of 11 I have been living in Germany. At first I was a computer scientist, but soon I realized that I was meant to become an artist. So I quit my job and plunged headlong into my new life.

Manga was my artistic start and not only got me into drawing, but also inspired me to live in Japan for a year and a half. The diligence and dedication that artists need to draw manga and anime still impress me.
For several years I drew manga intensively and published short stories in anthologies with other artists. This was followed, among other things, by background work for a 2D feature film and work as a concept artist in the gaming industry.

Today I am booked throughout Europe as a portrait artist. Simultaneously, I've been working as a lecturer for schools, academies and other institutions for about 15 years now. Through my regular manga courses in particular, a lot of material has accumulated, so I thought to myself: Now is the time to bring out this knowledge as a book!

All my experience from the different artistic careers and the love for drawing are in this book. I wish you a lot of creative fun!

MAXIM

BEFORE WE START:

Before you dive into the contents of this book full of motivation, I would like to briefly explain how I built the "School of Manga". This will help you better understand my methods and at the same time you will experience greater learning success.

For more than 15 years I have been giving drawing lessons on a variety of topics. But of course I also learned to draw once myself. This book is therefore based on my own experiences as a drawing student on the one hand and on my experiences as a teacher on the other hand.

NUMBERING

To help you find your way around, the individual drawing steps per exercise are usually numbered. Sometimes, however, I have omitted the numbers because they would unnecessarily overload the pages in some places. In these cases, always orient yourself from left to right per line, as if you were reading a text, and follow the pictures from top left to bottom right. Of course, the corresponding text will always help you follow the individual steps in the correct order.

INTRODUCTION

TIPS FOR USING THIS BOOK

PUMP UP YOUR CREATIVE BICEPS STEP BY STEP

Maybe you've already noticed: drawing manga is a mammoth task – especially if you want to draw your own stories someday. For this you have to take over the tasks of a director, a writer, a drawer and a layouter all at the same time. All of these are professions that take years or even decades to learn. But this challenge is so motivating! The task of developing a beautiful drawing or story rewards you with an exhilarating feeling of having created something great.

Now, of course, the question arises: how do I reach this point where I no longer have to struggle with drawing challenges and can instead fully concentrate on my artistic vision?

The answer is: go step by step and take enough time for the basics. Sure, you'd like to get started right away and draw a cool pose in perspective. But you'll quickly realize that it's not that easy. Drawing not only takes time, drawing requires a strong foundation. Of course, you shouldn't lose your fun in drawing by just practicing non-stop. But you should practice regularly and always acquire new knowledge.

That's how you constantly get better!

STEP 1: EYES, NOSE, EARS, MOUTH AND HAIR

In weightlifting, it's quite clear: before you reach for the heaviest dumbbell, you start with the light weights. It's the same with drawing. Drawing a whole character in perspective and movement is very difficult. That's why in this book we start by drawing the eyes, ears, mouth and nose. We pick out small areas and gradually build up our creative biceps.

STEP 2: FACES FROM THREE STANDARD PERSPECTIVES

Once the drawing of the eyes and the other components of the face is successful, our creative biceps are ready to draw a complete face – without perspective and facial expressions, of course! A "simple" face is challenge enough at first! When it comes to faces, I now further differentiate between styles and difficulty levels.

CHIBI

SHOJO/SHONEN

SEINEN/JOSEI

The *chibi* drawing style is extremely cute and highly simplified. I like to use this style to explain the first basics. Especially for beginners, the *chibi* style is a perfect introduction

The *shojo* and *shonen* style is probably the best known manga style in the western world. A large part of the well-known anime and manga are drawn in this style and are often aimed at teenagers through their aesthetic. Compared to *chibis*, the characters in this style seem more adult, but are still very simplified artistically.

Seinen and *josei* styles are aimed at a young adult audience. The characters in this style look more adult and realistic. Perfect for those whose creative biceps are calling for more of a challenge!

STEP 3: PERSPECTIVE, FACIAL EXPRESSIONS AND AGE LEVELS

If you've been diligent up to this point, your creative biceps are already pumped up – but possibly still a bit stiff and immobile.You can already lift a lot, but you can't yet react flexibly to different situations. For example, if someone knocks over a vase near you and you have to catch it with a quick reaction, your thick biceps won't help you much. Therefore, perspective and facial expressions are now added.

These two themes take advantage of the skills we've built up so far and make them flexible. After all, our goal is to eventually be able to draw any pose and any character. To do that, it's important to be versatile and not be limited by a lack of perspective, facial expressions, or construction methods. "Be water, my friend!"

STEP 4: HEADGEAR AND SHADING

We can now draw the "naked" head flexibly. But characters experience different weather conditions, ages and trends. They need head covers to protect their heads or make them prettier. Head covers are extensions of the head. Therefore, it is important to be confident in drawing heads before drawing over them.

TO CONCLUDE: DRAW A MANGA SHORT STORY

Now use the accumulated knowledge from the previous chapters. This way you'll learn twice as fast and strengthen your artistic skills.

Drawing a manga story is the ultimate drawing exercise for me.You're forced to use facial expressions and perspective. Also, you can't avoid drawing the same character from different perspectives. This "compulsion" to work on a story of my own, has always made me draw more than I was used to. I've done numerous short stories (about 20 pages and have improved immensely with each completed story.

Important: I don't explicitly go into how to create or structure a complete manga short story in this book. This is just a recommendation for you to try out if you're looking for a new way to practice after reading the book.

Another tip: Always set yourself your own challenges. I like to divide it up so that I only draw eyes for a week, for example, or different hairstyles for a week. In doing so, I gather a lot of references about different eye parts, hair types, interesting angles, etc. By focusing on one specific thing for a longer period of time, I improve all the faster. To constantly get better, you need structure and a plan.

Try it sometime! But never lose your fun in drawing. If you don't like a drawing exercise, feel free to change it so that you enjoy it again. Be creative! It's harder to learn without joy.

HOW IMPORTANT IS THE MANGA DRAWING STYLE?

We've already touched on a few manga styles above: *chibi, shojo/ shonen, seinen/josei*. Every manga artist who draws in these styles automatically adds a personal touch. Thus, these general styles give rise to an almost infinite number of different variations.

There is generally a lot of discussion about manga styles! Sure, they are important. It often depends on the style whether you find a manga or anime especially cool. But how important is the drawing style for an artist?

If you want to learn to draw, then the question of style – especially in the beginning – is irrelevant. First of all, it is important to learn the basics, the foundation of drawing. It's elementary to understand that behind every drawing style are the same fundamental principles. Whether you're drawing very simplified chibistyle characters or painting a highly realistic portrait, you're dealing with human-like characters.

The same principles apply to them. If you improve your sense of proportion, your knowledge of anatomy, and your three-dimensional understanding, then you can learn to draw in all kinds of styles.

It is also important to understand that manga is simplified and stylized reality. This means that reality must first be studied in order to understand how to draw it in a simplified way. Of course, too much theory would take the fun out of drawing for many beginners.

If drawing manga motivates you, then draw manga! The more you draw, the more you improve your skills. What exactly you draw is secondary. But if you want to become a really good artist someday, you can't avoid drawing reality and studying it.

These four drawings of mine do not represent an artistic development over time, as it might seem at first glance. Instead, I used my knowledge to consciously apply different drawing styles. After all, if you learn the basics, you can jump back and forth between different styles much more easily.

FINDING YOUR OWN DRAWING STYLE

The search for your own style is an exciting journey. What is your own style? When did you find it? Well, I find that one's style reflects one's personality and current knowledge.

This means that as you grow personally and expand your knowledge, your style will adapt. That's completely normal. And the bottom line is this: every picture you draw is drawn in your style. Because your personality flows into every stroke you make, making every stroke completely unique. Don't search so much for your style, but improve in your drawing. The more confident you feel, the more likely your own style will come to you.

Exercises to get better at drawing arms and hands. As a course instructor and book author, I naturally try to appeal to as many people as possible. To do this, I use examples from different manga styles. I want to convey the artistic techniques behind these styles – as far as this is possible in a book. So my recommendation is: even if in your favorite manga or anime the eyes are drawn a little differently, for example, still try to go through the exercises in this book at least once. They will help you improve your drawing skills.

IMPORTANT TIP:

Do not just read the text, but try to draw along with ALL the exercises if possible.

Exercises to get better at drawing arms and hands.

The exercises in this book can basically be done with all drawing materials. What I want to teach, however, is not so much how exactly you draw with pencil or how you alternatively draw digitally. Rather, you should build a basic understanding of things like proportions, anatomy and shading. What drawing materials you work with is entirely up to you. Nevertheless, I would like to give you a few tips on how to best use this book - both for digital drawing and for drawing with pencil.

CHAPTER 1

DRAWING MATERIALS

1.1 TIPS FOR DIGITAL DRAWING

THE ONE BRUSH I USE TO DRAW EVERYTHING IN THIS BOOK

I have drawn almost all the drawings in this book digitally. For me, this is the perfect method to convey my knowledge neatly. For this I have always used the same brush: In the Photoshop program, this default brush is called "Hard Round Pressure Size."
In the popular alternative Procreate, it would be the brush "Calligraphy -> Script". These two digital brushes change size depending on the pressure. They have a hard edge and are very similar to an ink pen.

I also draw the shadows with this setting.

DRAWING SOFTWARE AND TABLET

I use only basic functions of my drawing software that are also available in all other popular drawing applications. Unfortunately, detailed explanations for each of these tools are beyond the scope of this book.

Basically, you can draw with any kind of graphics tablet. In my opinion, it's just important that it's not too small. If the strokes you draw are too wobbly at first, look for the function in your drawing program that smoothes the lines. With this little "cheat" you can improve the quality of your drawings immensely.

THIS IS HOW I CONSTRUCT MY DRAWINGS IN A DIGITAL DRAWING APP:

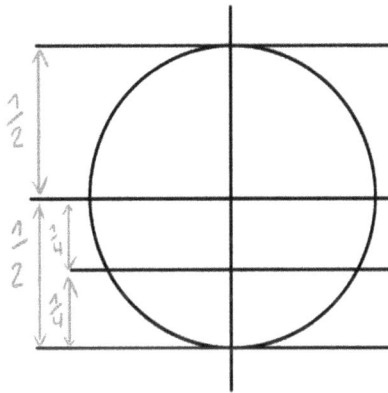

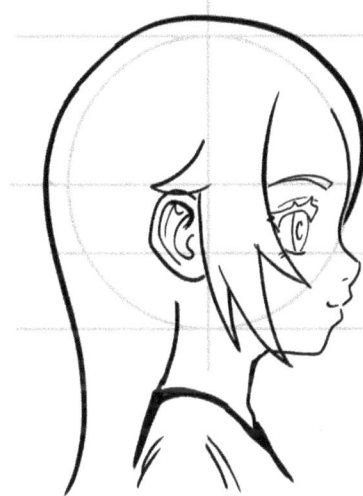

LAYER 1: THE STRUCTURE

We need the structure so that we have something for orientation. Something we can shimmy along and find the right proportions. I will hide this layer later, which is why I draw the construction lines on a separate layer.

LAYER 2: OUTLINES

I set the first layer to 30% opacity. This allows me to follow the structure, but it does not interfere with further drawing. Then I create a new layer above layer 1. On this layer 2 I draw clean outlines.

HIDE STRUCTURE LAYER

Once I have drawn most of the character, I hide layer 1 with the construction lines. This allows me to concentrate fully on completing the outlines.

LAYER 3: BASIC SHADING

I place the shading layer (3) over the outline layer (2). I then set the shading layer to "multiply". This makes the outlines show through, even though I draw the shading over the outlines.

LAYER 4:
BASIC DARK SHADE FOR THE HAIR

I create the basic dark shade for the hair on a fourth layer below the outline layer (2). I paint the hair with one shade of gray. The shading layer (3) automatically adjusts the shadows depending on which shades of grey I use.

LAYER 5:
BASIC DARK SHADE FOR THE CLOTHING

To make the clothes stand out from the skin, I fill in a t-shirt with a light gray tone, for example. Using many layers has several advantages. For example, since hair and clothing are each on their own layer, I could now adjust the darkness of the hair or clothing separately at any time.

LAYER 6:
HAIR HIGHLIGHTS

To give the hair shine and volume, I create another layer called "hair highlights" (layer 6). This layer is below the outline layer (2) and above the base color layer (4). First I draw just one stripe and erase some areas.

LAYER 7:
HAIR COLOR GRADIENT

For the gradient of the hair I use the gradient tool. To make the gradient work only on the hair, I need to create a clipping mask layer on the hair color layer (4). Check out some tutorials on the web for this. This feature is for advanced users, but it is super helpful.

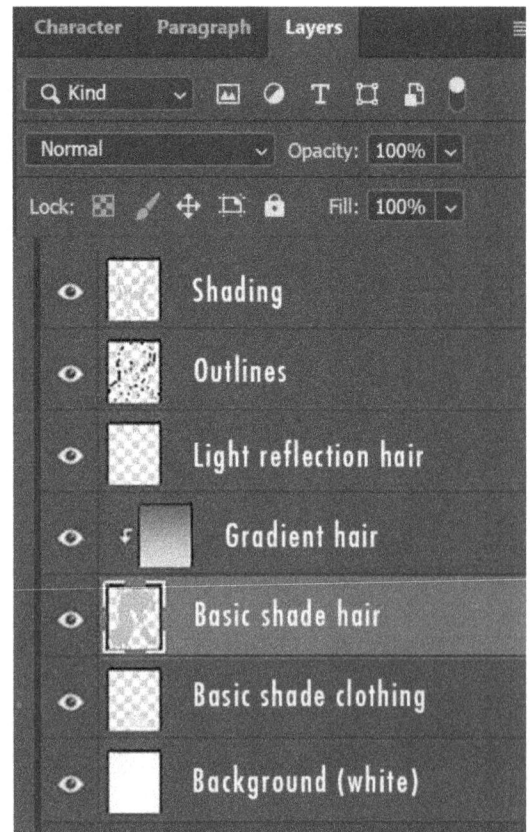

My arrangement of layers in Photoshop on a finished drawing

1.2 TIPS FOR DRAWING WITH PENCIL AND INK

Traditional drawing on paper has a charm that cannot be imitated.
Even though the professional artist world in the fields of manga, games
and movies now relies heavily on digital drawing, I still love to come back to
my sketchbooks and draw with pencil or ink. Especially when traveling, I have
tremendous fun filling one sketchbook after another and trying out many
different pens.

My sketchbook during a trip across Japan

EXERCISE: CIRCLE DRAWING AND HATCHING

In this book, many drawings start with a circle. Therefore, start by learning how to draw a relatively symmetrical circle. Practice makes perfect, so don't be afraid to draw 10 or 100 or even 1000 circles. It doesn't have to be a perfect circle, but the shape should at least be clean and relatively symmetrical. Next, practice hatching. This will help you create gradients and can further enhance your manga drawings.

1.Try your hand at these shapes and hatch them cleanly - with or without gradient :)

2.Hatch this shape with parallel lines. Make sure that the lines stay within the shape.

3. Or hatch the shape so that it is neatly filled and balanced.

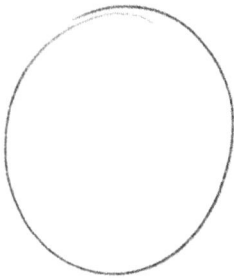

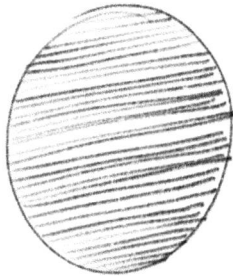

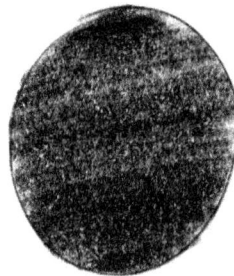

4. Hatch the shape with a gradient.Try to create as soft a gradient as possible.

Try out these shapes and hatch them cleanly – with or without gradient. :)

In this book I have mainly drawn digitally. If you draw in pencil, make sure that you only press down very lightly and use hard pencils, especially for the preliminary drawing (i.e. the structure).

When you draw the finished outlines, you can press harder and use softer pencils. Or you can use ink. Once the ink is dry, you can easily erase the pencil outline.

Shading is an advanced drawing technique. Therefore, practice drawing clean lines and shapes first.
It is important that the proportions are correct.

As soon as the outline drawing becomes easy to do, more and more shadows can be added little by little. I explain briefly the placement of the shadows in this book, but I do not go into the depths. This would simply be too advanced and I would need another 200 pages *laughs*.

Therefore, with this book, focus especially on practicing outlines and proportions.

Eyes, nose, ears and lips are their own complex and totally individual areas on the head. It is therefore worth looking at these areas in detail first and becoming more confident in drawing them.

The more practice and confidence you have in drawing ears, for example, the more fun and relaxed it will be to draw a complete character. This way you avoid frustration with small details and can direct all your creative energy to the complete expression of the character.

CHAPTER 2

HOW TO DRAW EYES, EARS, LIPS & NOSE

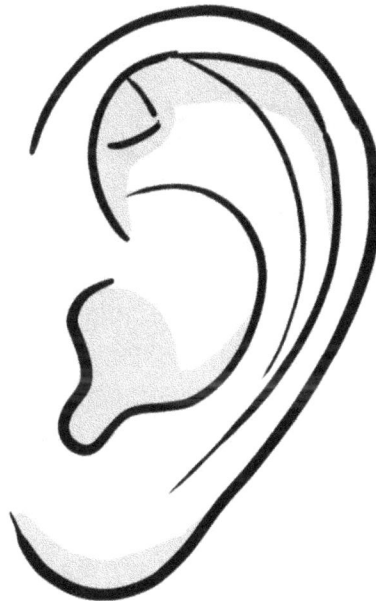

2.1 DRAWING EYES STEP BY STEP

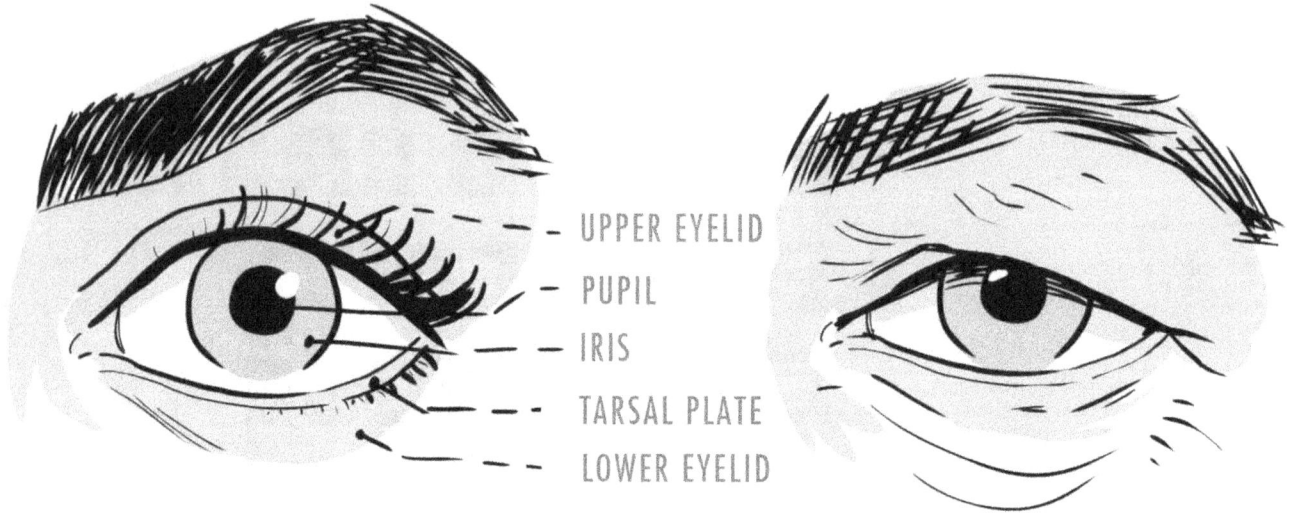

UPPER EYELID
PUPIL
IRIS
TARSAL PLATE
LOWER EYELID

The eye has a special status not only in manga. The eyes also play an important role in realistic drawing or simply in personal interaction between two people. That's why many artists start with drawing the eyes.

The manga eye is built on the same principle as the real eye. First, let's look step by step at how a relatively realistic eye is drawn:

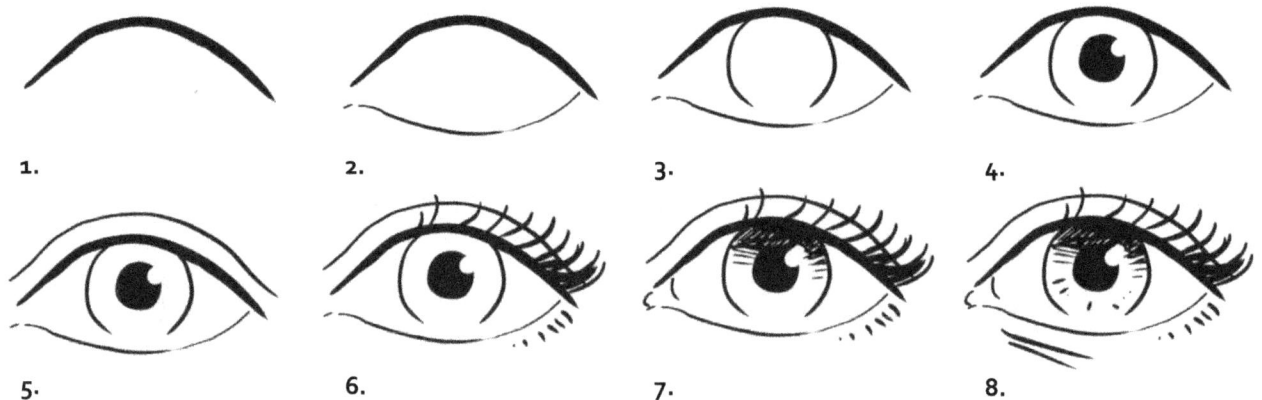

1.

2.

3.

4.

5.

6.

7.

8.

1. Draw the line for the upper eyelid. It is rather thick and strongly curved, almost like a roof shape.

2. The line of the lower eyelid is thinner and not as rounded as the upper eyelid.

3. The iris

4. The pupil with a light spot

5. The eyelid crease runs parallel to the line of the upper eyelid

6. Eyelashes

7. Shadow cast by the upper eyelid on the iris

8. The iris starts dark and becomes lighter towards the bottom.

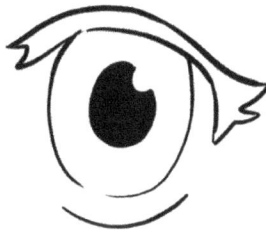

With the manga eye, we basically proceed in exactly the same way as with the real eye. The shapes are slightly different, but the individual elements remain the same. A manga eye is special, but ultimately it is the stylized form of a realistic eye.

Here, too, the upper eyelid is drawn particularly thick and expansive. The lower eyelid remains thin and inconspicuous. The line of the iris starts stronger and becomes interrupted and thinner towards the bottom.

Parallel to the upper eyelid, the eyelid crease (line at the very top) is drawn. This gives the eye more shape. The eyelashes are refined. Draw them sometimes in larger clumps and sometimes in smaller ones.

The eyebrow has a good distance from the crease of the eyelid. The shape curves parallel around the eye.
The eyebrow starts out a little thicker and then becomes thinner and thinner. Of course, there are all kinds of eyebrow shapes. This shape is often used for shojo girls.
A free-floating pupil looks somewhat bizarre. Therefore, it is important to connect the upper eyelid to the pupil with the help of a shadow. This relaxes the eye. The upper eyelid casts a shadow on the iris and the eye itself.

The dark area of the iris is a perfect place for light spots. A completely white one must not be missing. My special tip: Draw a darkened light reflex in the shadow of the iris on the other side of the white light reflex. This makes the eye even more vivid!

1

Next, let's draw an eye in shonen style. Start with the outer shape of the eye. Pay attention to the angularity of the upper eyelid. Eyelashes are only slightly indicated on the left.

2

The eyebrow hangs low over the eye. It even overlaps the eye at the upper left corner. To make the eyebrow a little bushier, add thin strokes at both ends.

3

Now add the iris and the pupil. The gaze is focused and tense. The iris is partially covered by the upper eyelid. The pupil is small and conveys alertness.

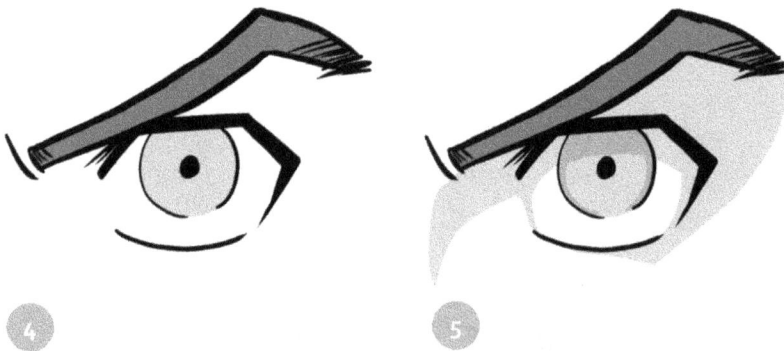

4

5

Choose a light shade for the iris as a foundation. Build a large shadow area around the eye. The iris gets a darker shadow in the upper area and a darker outer edge.

6

The eyebrow can be drawn black or – as in this case – very dark. This makes it stand out well from the shadow underneath.

Shading on the white of the eye gives it a lot of depth and roundness. Now it's just a matter of adding a light point and a few strokes (pointing to the pupil) to the iris to give the eye more vibrancy.

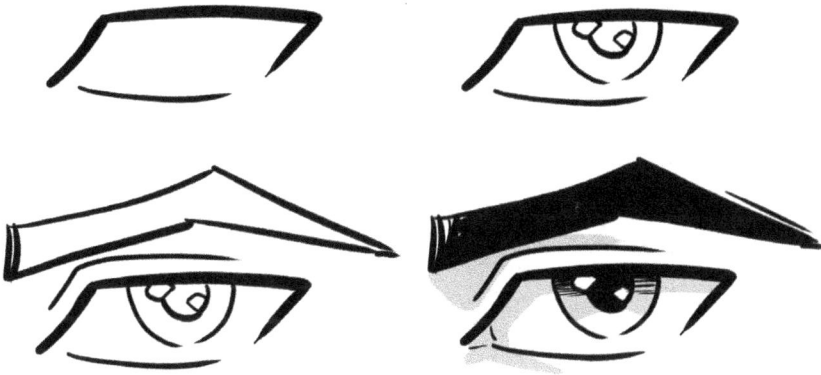

This eye and the eyebrow are some-what sharper in their shape. This makes the character look more serious and cool.

The upper areas of the pupil and iris are more covered by the upper eyelid. The eyebrow is very close to the eye.

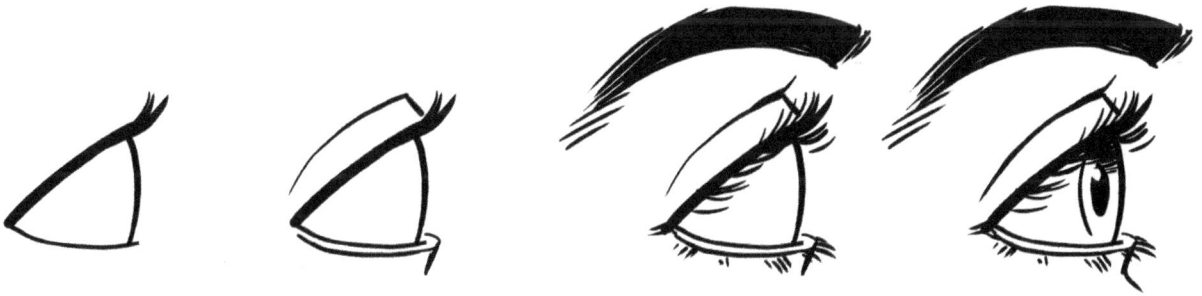

The eye from the side starts with a shape reminiscent of a triangle. Note that the lines around the eye and the line of the eye itself are rounded. After all, the eye is a sphere. The upper and lower eyelids have a certain thickness. Therefore, they are drawn slightly past the eyeball. The pupil of the real eye does not lie on the outside of the eyeball, but lies slightly inside the eye.

In manga drawings, this fact is often ignored because it is easier to place the pupil directly on the edge of the eye. It then looks a bit doll-like, as if the pupil had simply been glued onto the eye at the end. Sometimes, though, it's exactly this "doll-like" aesthetic that fits the style. It is not a huge difference. So decide for yourself which technique you want to use.

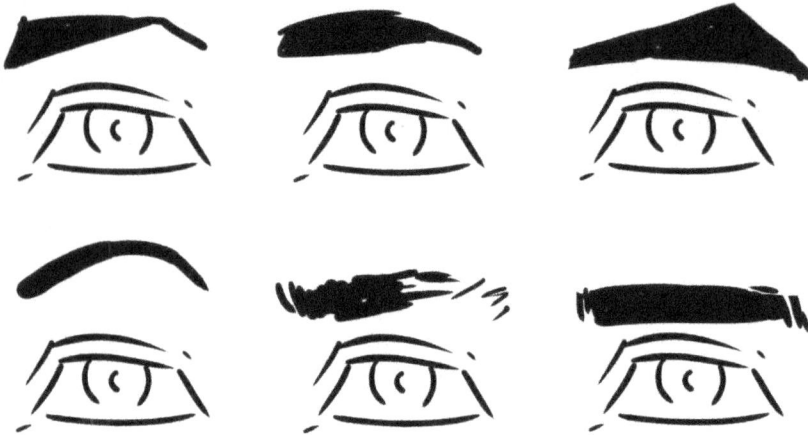

The influence of the eyebrows should not be underestimated. They strongly shape the visual appearance of a character.

Observe your surroundings or take note in mangas of which characters get which types of eyebrows.

We will address perspective drawing in more detail in a separate chapter. But we can already start with a preliminary exercise. You can never practice too much perspective.

Seen from below, the eye bulges upward - especially the upper eyelid. You can see the thickness of the upper eyelid. The lower eyelid is drawn almost straight with a slight bulge.

The eyebrow arches particularly strongly upward and gains distance to the eye. The pupil is compressed, no longer as round as seen directly from the front.

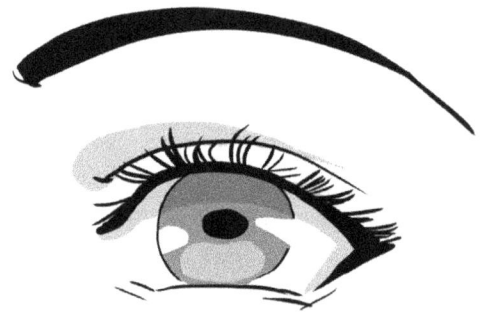

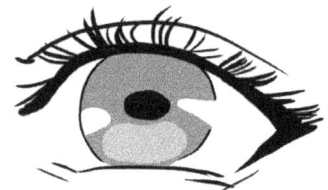

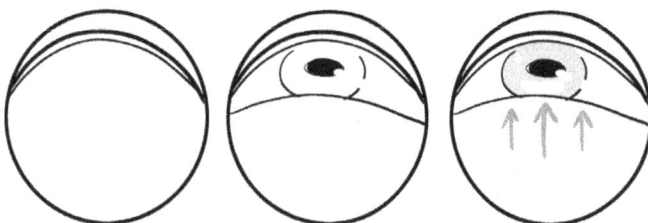

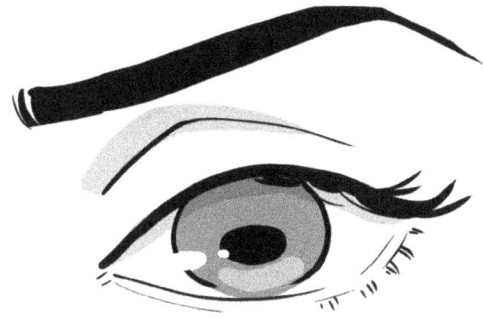

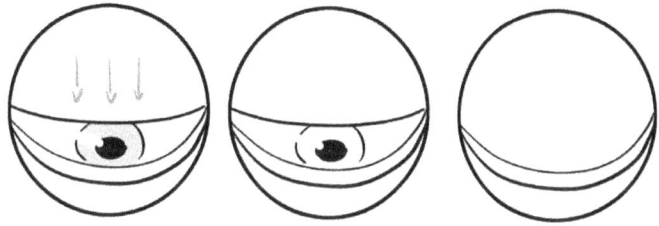

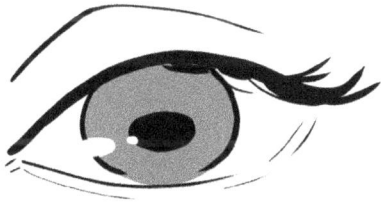

In the view from above, exactly the opposite happens. The upper eyelid becomes flatter and the lower eyelid shows a clear downward bulge. You can also clearly see the thickness of the lower eyelid.

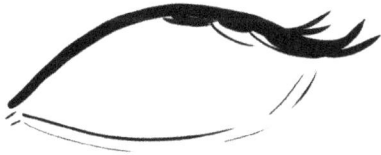

The pupil is compressed, no longer circular and slips down a bit. The eyebrow appears somewhat "flatter" and is closer to the eye. The eyelashes now protrude more into the eye. This technique is very helpful in establishing perspective.

Also, draw the highlights a little further down.

Although the *shonen* eye is drawn in a very simplified way, the same structure applies as with the realistic eye.

The better you can draw an eye in different styles and the better you understand the real anatomy of the eye, the easier it will be to draw.

2.2 DRAWING EARS STEP BY STEP

An ear has quite complex shapes that all interlock. However, when you get to know the individual shapes and work out the ear several times, you start to see a pattern behind it. I think it's totally worthwhile to study the ear. It's importance is often underestimated. A detailed ear is quickly drawn and adds a lot of vibrancy to the character.

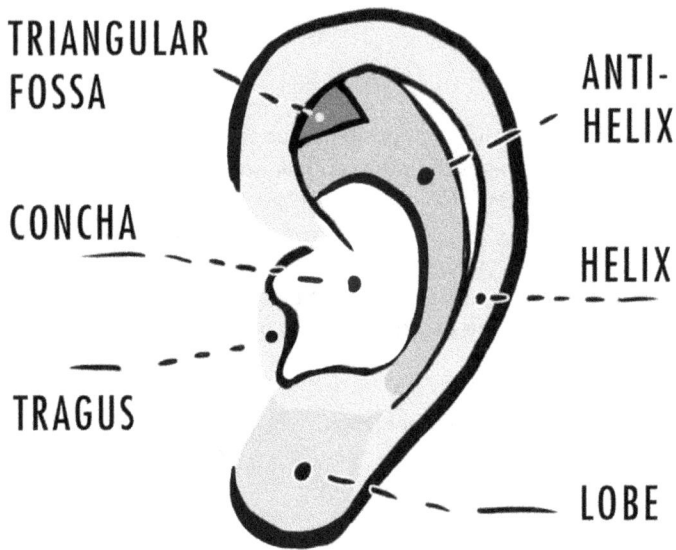

TRIANGULAR FOSSA

ANTI-HELIX

CONCHA

HELIX

TRAGUS

LOBE

Of course, you do not have to learn the individual anatomical terms by heart. It is only important that you have heard them at least once. When drawing ears, you will later unconsciously look for these shapes and thus be able to draw more authentic ears. Especially for setting shadows, knowledge of anatomy is a must.

First draw the line where the ear is attached (dashed line). The ear is often attached to the head at an angle and has the shape of a 9.

The upper part of the ear is quite round.You could use a circle as an auxiliary shape here. From the circle, the ear becomes a bit flatter and finally ends in the earlobe.

Start with the helix so that you have the outer shape of the ear complete.

1

2

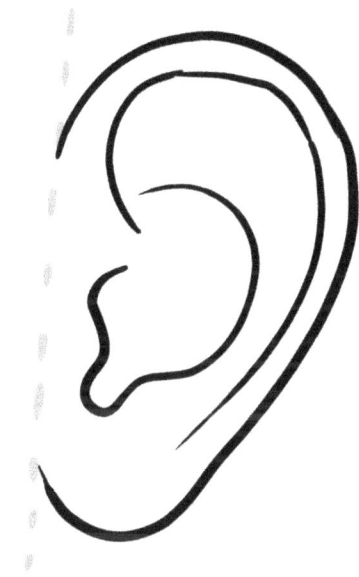

3

Now draw the line around the conchal cavity. This line includes the tragus and the antitragus (bulge opposite the tragus). The line also defines one side of the anti-helix.

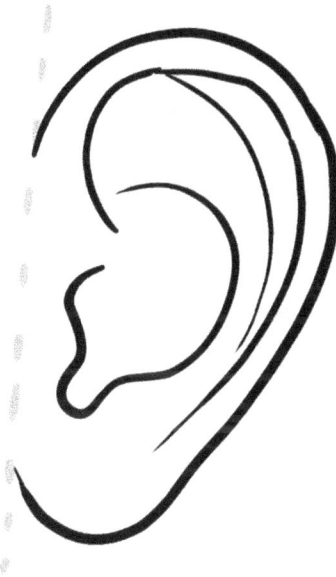

4

Next, draw the right side of the anti-helix. Initially the anti-helix has some distance to the helix, but towards the bottom the two shapes nestle together.

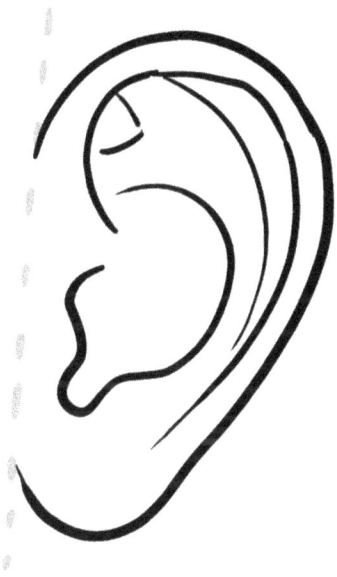

5

The earlobe does not need to be defined separately. We already do this with the outer line and by leaving room for the earlobe in all other lines. Finally, the triangular fossa at the top!

6

If you feel bold, draw in some shading. Especially the upper area of the helix casts a shadow. And of course also at the tragus, because where the ear canal begins, it is darker.

The ear from behind often appears when you draw a manga story and two characters are talking. Then you see the back of one character's head in the foreground.

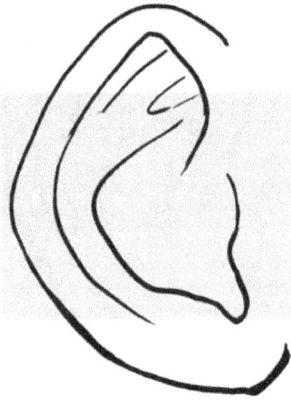

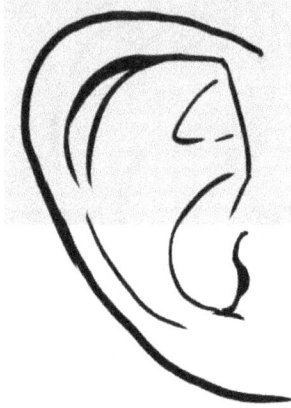

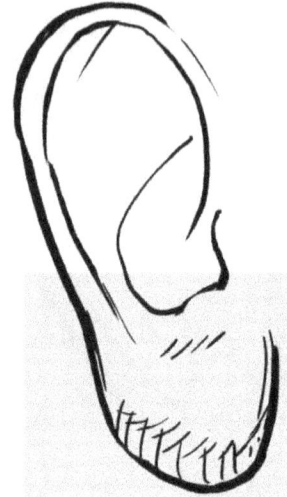

In the beginning it is good to practice the ear again and again with the "9-method" until you can draw it from memory without any problems.

The next step is to recognize that ears can have very different shapes. Sometimes the middle part of an ear is emphasized, sometimes the upper part, and sometimes the earlobe is so large that the upper shape of the ear is totally eclipsed.

Ears also have their own unique character and therefore have a great influence on a person's appearance. Therefore, choose the ear shape of your manga characters consciously.

The cup handle always reminds me of an ear! XD

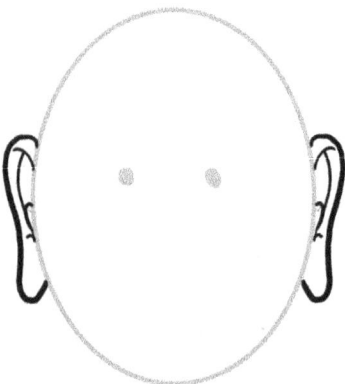

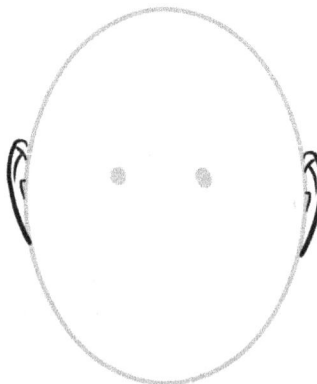

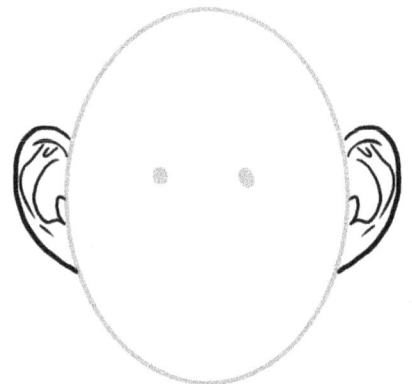

Discrete, protruding, small and large ears

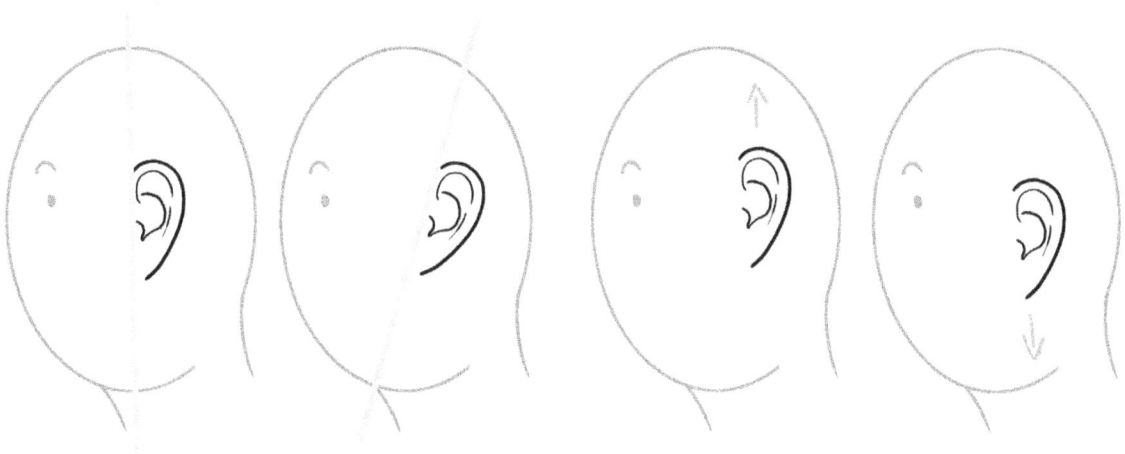

It is often said that the ear is aligned with the height of the nose.
But in reality, the ear behaves as it wants.

Sometimes it lies very low, sometimes it slides up, sometimes it is super slanted, sometimes very straight. This is completely independent of the nose or the eyes. Learn the "standard proportions" first, but always keep in mind that there is no such thing as "standard" at this point. This flexibility will improve your character design immensely.

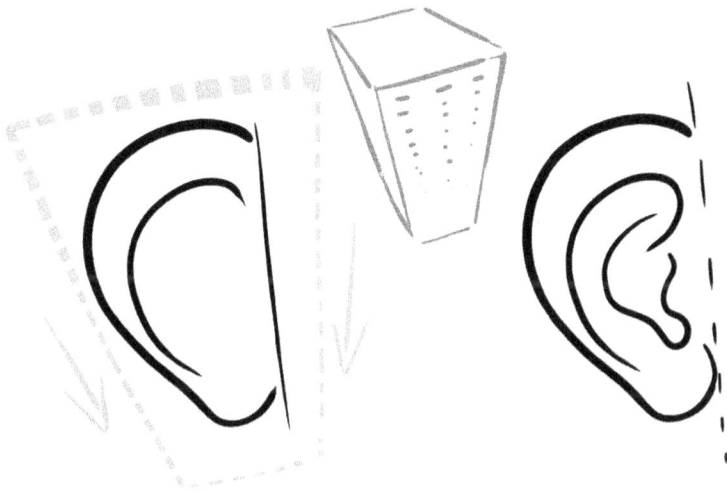

When you look at an ear from above, you can see the upper part of the helix in particular. In this case the earlobe is rather unimportant, just like the rest of the shapes further down.

Imagine looking at a house from above. You will mainly see the roof. All details disappear towards the bottom and will become more indistinct.

The opposite is true for the ear seen from below. Here the earlobe is in the foreground and can be emphasized more clearly with a thicker line. The helix at the top and the rest of the upper shapes of the ear are less important.

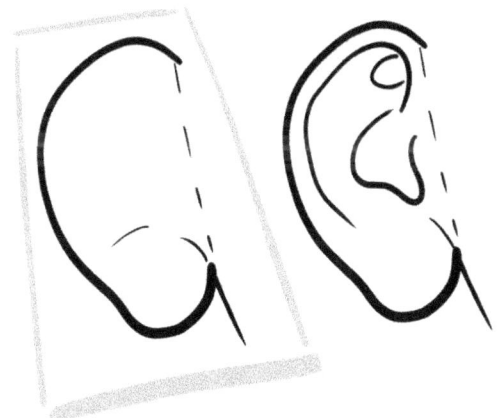

2.3 DRAWING NOSES STEP BY STEP

The nose is often particularly simplified in manga stories. Sometimes it is even omitted altogether. Even if the nose thus seems to be very secondary for manga drawing, it is immensely important to also get to know this body part in its real form. The manga noses, although highly simplified, also follow the principles of the real nose.

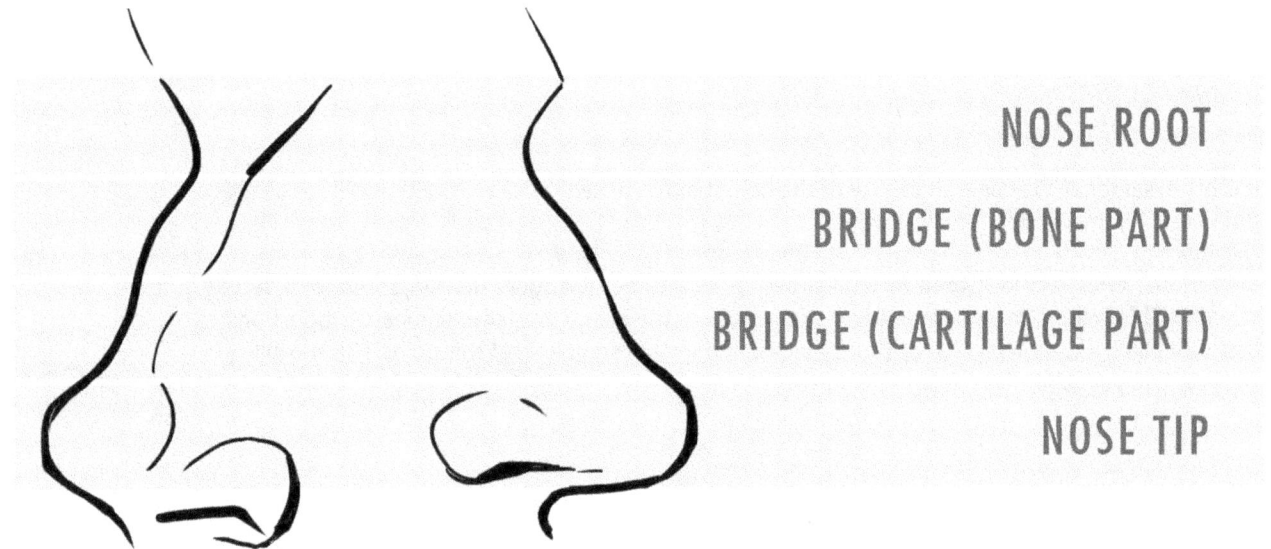

NOSE ROOT

BRIDGE (BONE PART)

BRIDGE (CARTILAGE PART)

NOSE TIP

The same character, but with a different nose each time, looks like a completely different person. Here you can see at first glance how the nose affects the visual impression of a character. In manga, noses often all look the same, but good manga artists draw slight differences in length and position.You simply need different noses for different characters. To notice these subtle differences, it is important to exaggerate and draw "extreme" nose shapes in the beginning. Try it! It's fun! :D

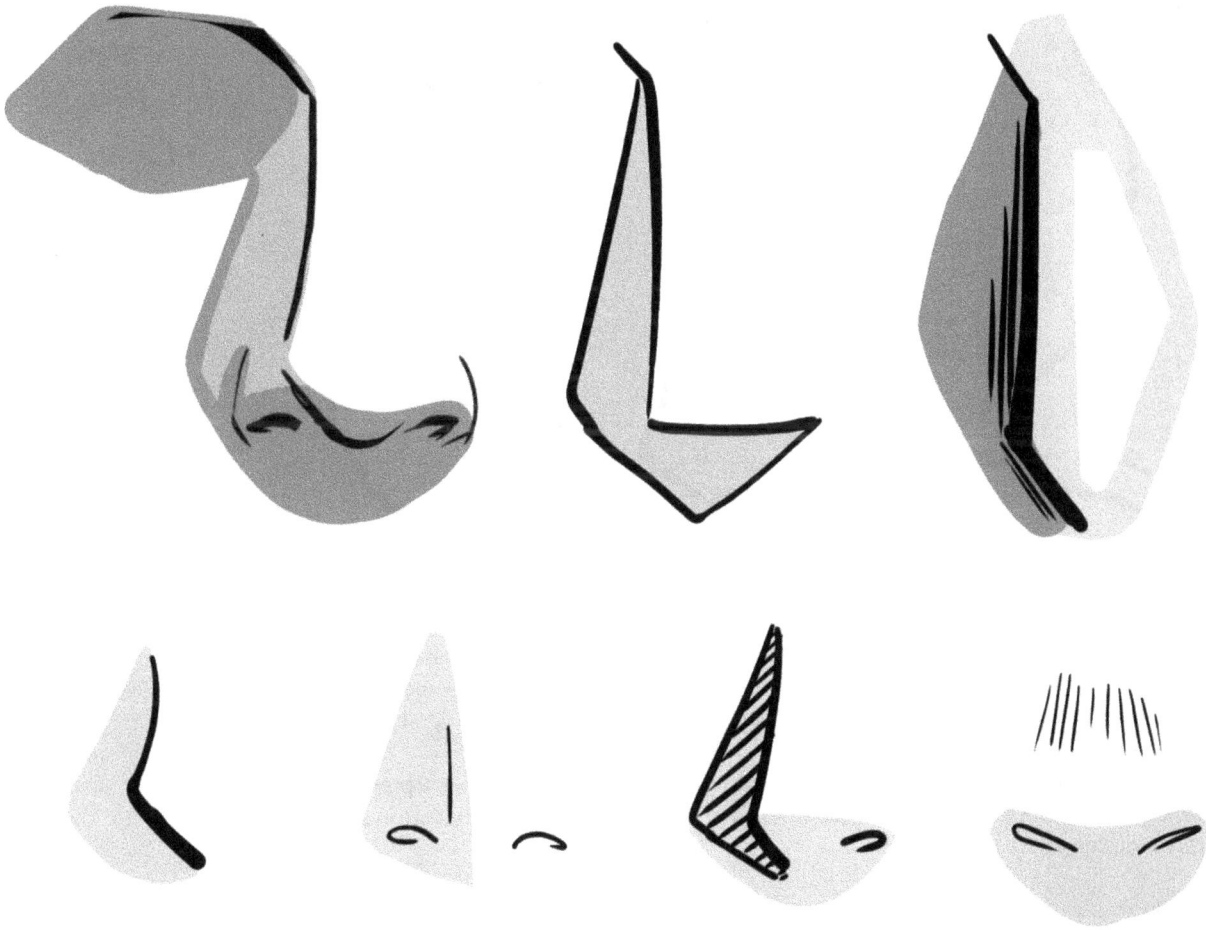

Various styles of displaying the nose from the front. All examples look different, but are subject to the same principle. Draw all the noses. Which shadows and lines are repeated? The line of the nose originates from the eyebrow. Since the nose protrudes from the face, it casts a shadow on the face. The shadow under the nose and the shadow on one side of the nose are important and are often used in manga. Which manga nose drawing style do you prefer?

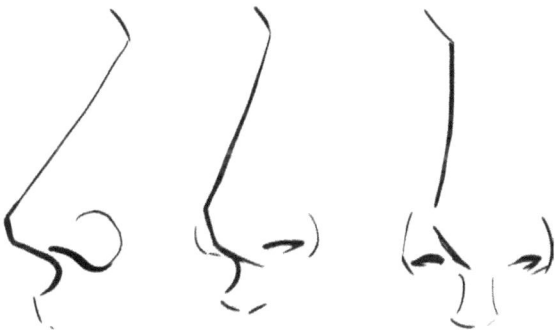

The sides of the nose are relatively difficult to draw, although they have a simple shape. In manga, they are usually omitted, while the nostrils are drawn in. Try to practice drawing realistic noses from different perspectives. That way you'll be able to draw simplified noses much easier.

The typical *shojo* manga style has only small poke noses, comparable to the first nose shape in this example. This is certainly due to the fact that most people in Japan have rather inconspicuous noses. That's why the shojo style is super fitting for Japan.

As soon as non-Japanese people appear in manga books, they suddenly get very pronounced noses. But whether set in Japan or not, there are all kinds of different noseshapes that are important for character design.

The bridge between the eyebrows and the nose is important. With the character below, it wasn't enough to just change the nose. Only when I drew eyebrows that matched the noses did the face look more coherent.

2.4 DRAWING THE MOUTH STEP BY STEP

Whether a mouth is wide or narrow depends on the relationships of the individual facial elements to one another. When drawing the mouth in the front view, the pupils are usually used as a guide.

In manga, artists like to draw a rather narrow mouth. This looks very cute. The character then is no "big mouth". Here, too, it is important to get to know different mouth shapes and to consciously use this to suit the character. Mouths that are wider than the distance between the pupils can be considered large.

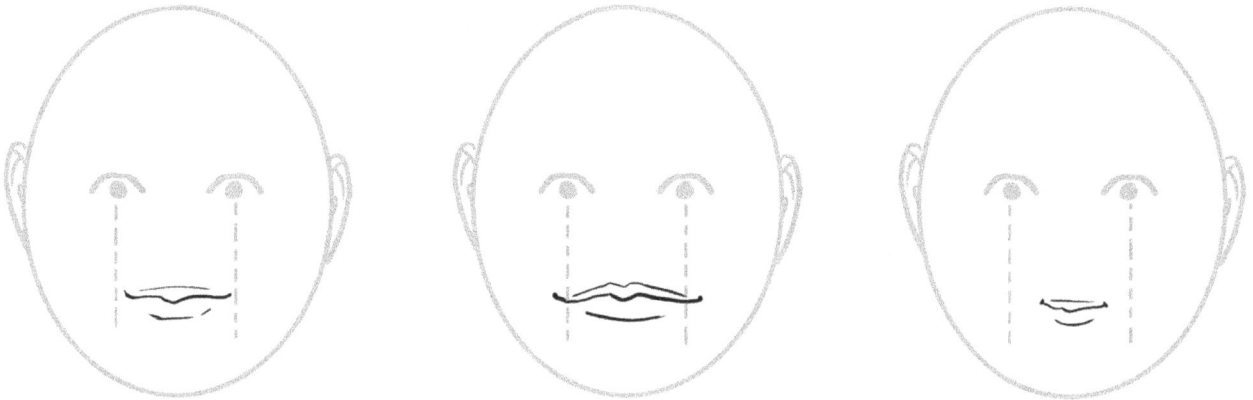

Since the light mostly comes from above (e.g. from the sun), the upper lip is drawn lying in the shadow. The lower lip is then more illuminated and remains lighter. In some manga styles, the lower lip is left out entirely, which still looks believable. The mouth says a lot about the character's disposition. Therefore, even with the mouth, create a collection of different shapes.

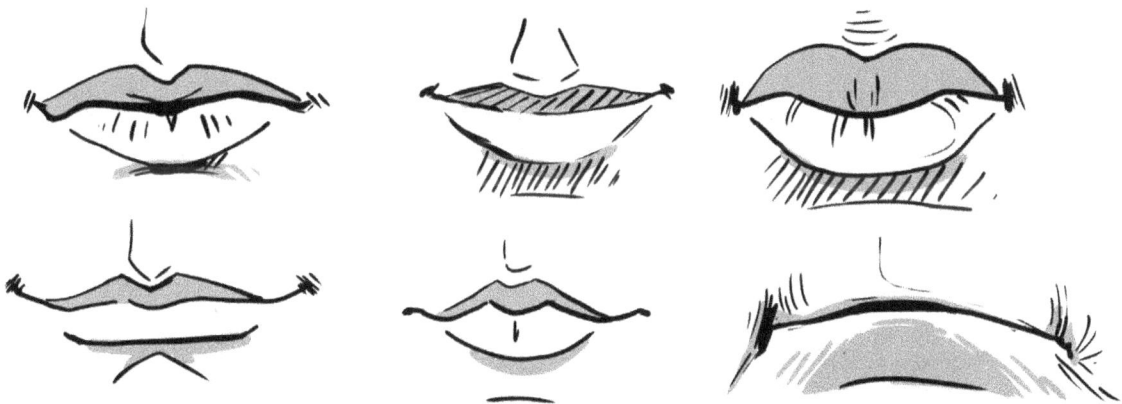

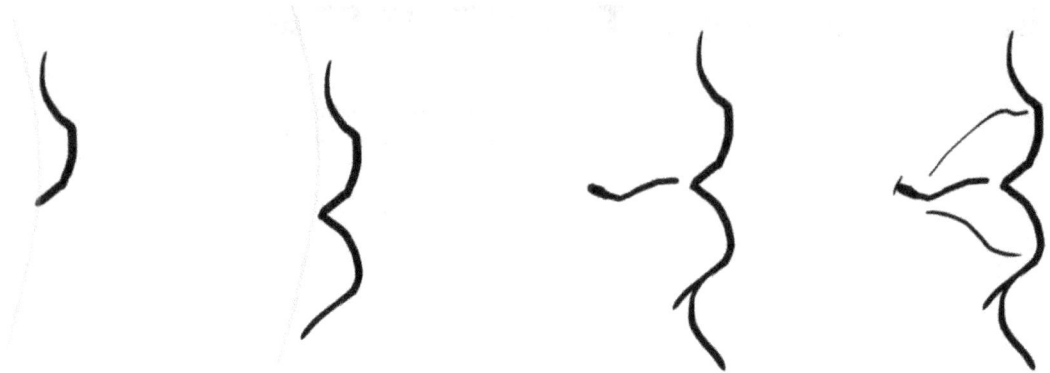

The lips are not simply round. Especially when viewed from the side, they are rather angular. The lip line is shaped like a staircase that consists of many extensions. Start with the upper lip and add the lower lip.

The line that defines the smile has some distance from the lip line. The lines for the upper and lower lip are quite thin. The ends do not touch the other lines. As a result, the lips do not look like they are painted on.

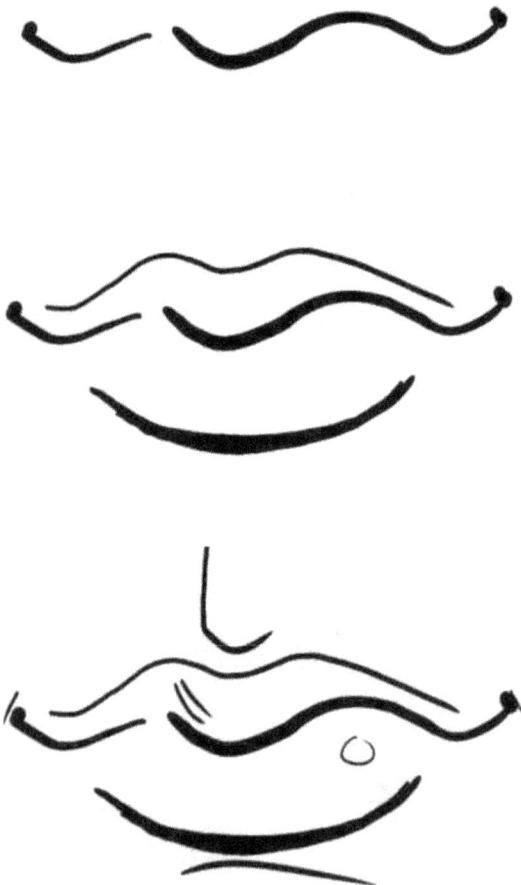

For the front view, I like to start with the middle line of the mouth. This often reminds me of a flying bird. The line is not completely continuous, but has a slight interruption.

In the second step, I add the lines for the upper and lower lip. Note that these lines do not touch the center line. Also, the upper line is much thinner than the lower one.

In the third step, I indicate the philtrum (the vertical groove between the nose and upper lip). I also draw in the base of the chin. Especially with the mouth, it's important to have lots of breaks in the lines. The trick to simplifying is to let the viewer complete the rest of the image in their mind. For this to be possible, there needs to be a lot of empty areas.

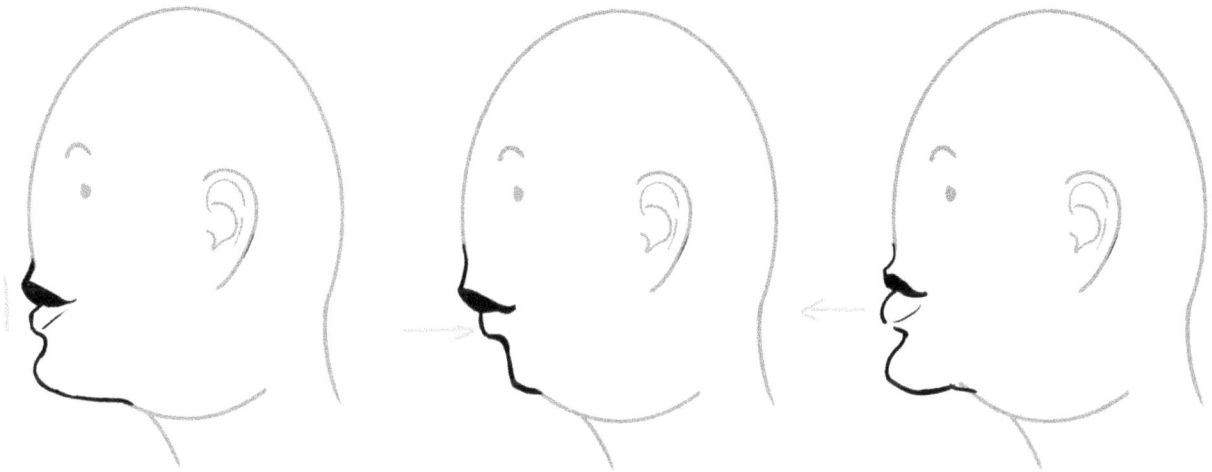

The mouth in the profile view reveals different character traits. Does the upper lip or the lower lip dominate? How pronounced is the chin? Let the differences in the illustration above work on you. How do they change the character? For your own characters, consciously choose the position of the lips and chin because it makes a big difference in visual expression.

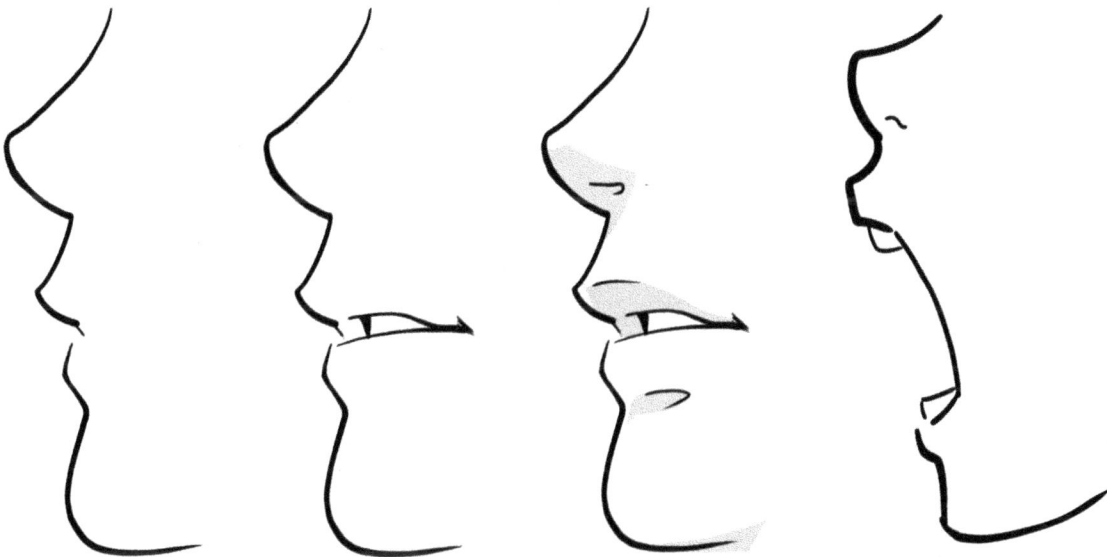

Usually shading is done below the nose, the upper lip, below the lower lip and below the chin. Often you have light coming from above and these are the areas that "turn away" from the light. Lighter shading is much better for adding depth to lips than black lines, for example. Because outer lines quickly make lips look "pasted on". Give the lips plenty of room to breathe.

When the mouth is opened, the lower jaw shifts not only downward but also slightly to the side (in this case to the right). The tense mouth line is oblique and you can see the beginnings of the teeth.

PALATE

UVULA

CANINE
TOOTH

GUMS

WISDOM TOOTH

PREMOLAR AND
MOLAR TEETH

INCISOR TEETH

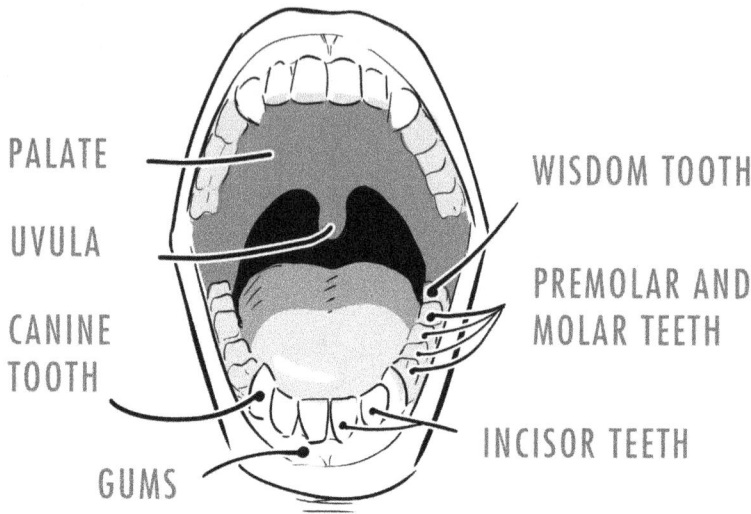

To give the teeth depth, leave the front incisors and canines light. The back molars and wisdom teeth are drawn in shadow. From the upper part of the mouth, the shadow falls on the tongue and the lower, back teeth. That is why the tongue has such a sharp-edged shadow at the back.

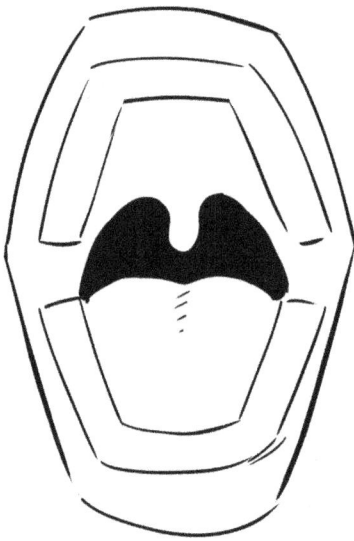

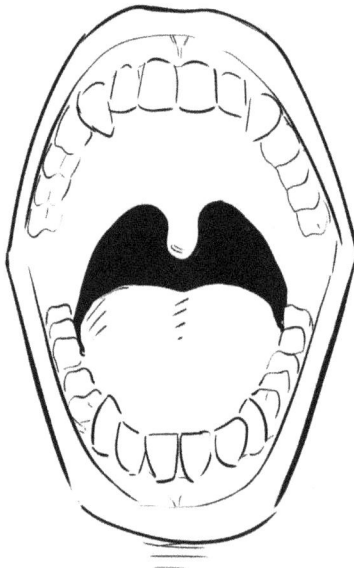

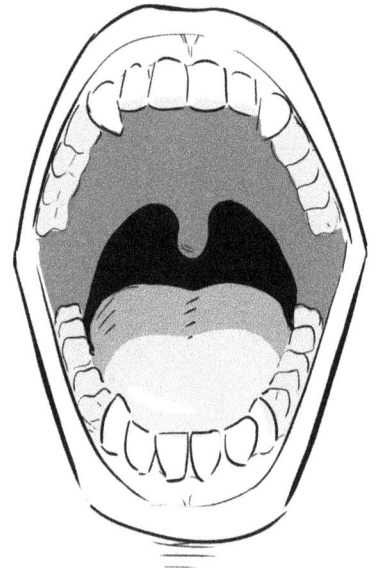

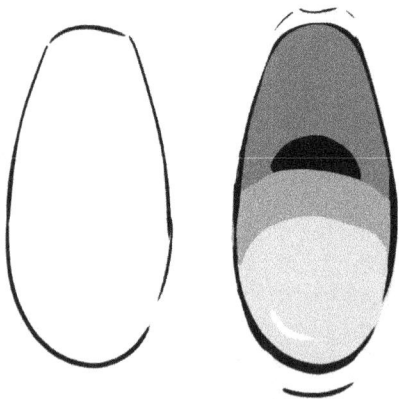

A highlight on the tongue can be drawn in, but is not mandatory. The tongue is wet and therefore predestined to have a highlight.

It is important to take a closer look at the mouth and to get to know it and its terminology. In manga, the mouth is often depicted in a very simplified way. The teeth, for example, are often omitted. You see the throat and only the tongue. Teeth are indeed difficult to draw. That is precisely why we should deal with them in more detail.

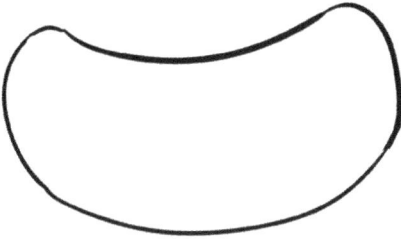

A grinning, open mouth shows teeth. If you want to draw a little more detail, first emphasize the space between the teeth and the outer mouth line on the left and right.

Indicate slight indentations in the center on the sides so that you can guess where the separation between the upper and lower row of teeth is.

With this shape, you can adjust the grin a bit and emphasize the canines. Note, however, that this will make the grin look a bit "meaner" or "more aggressive". It also depends on the character you are drawing. Sharp-edged teeth always give a more threatening expression.

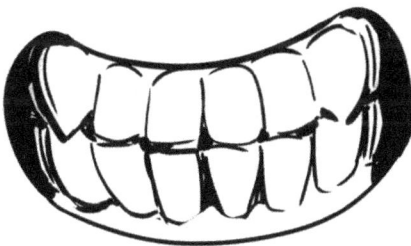

Sometimes you would like to draw every single tooth. But be careful: that can quickly become too "toothy" and remind you of a zombie mouth. Therefore, be more abstract and do not draw a dividing line between the individual teeth in a row.

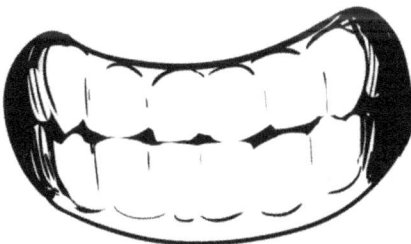

There may be an "uneven" parting line between rows of teeth, but not between individual teeth within a row.

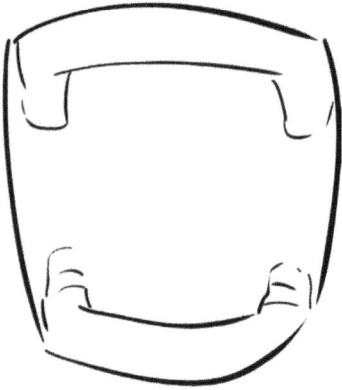
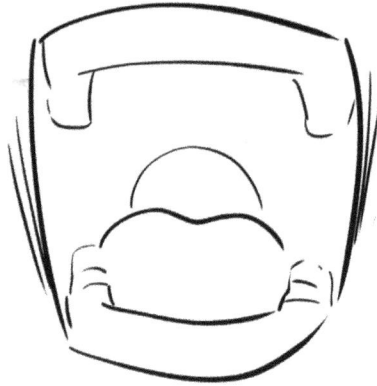
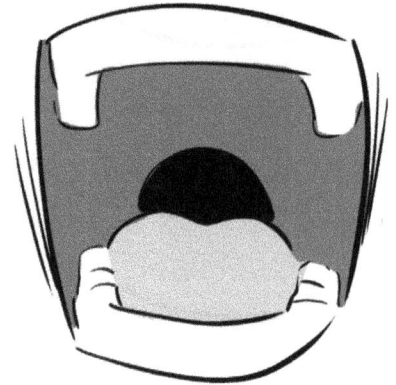

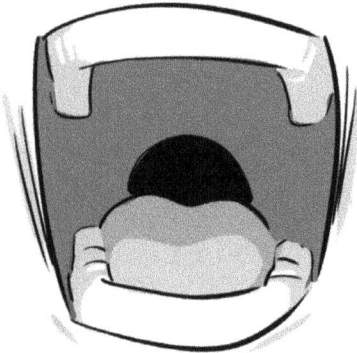

The teeth in manga often resemble a boxer's mouthguard.
The teeth merge into rows of teeth. The beauty of it: It looks good
and simplifies our drawing immensely.

For the back molars, you can hint at details with light cross strokes –
but not too much. Here, the front teeth are illuminated by the light, while
the back teeth are in the shadow of the mouth and appear darkened
accordingly.

In manga, sometimes only one canine tooth is drawn in. A mouth without teeth looks super friendly. After
all, you can't bite anyone without
teeth. The one canine tooth, on the
other hand, is an easy way to bring
back the "dangerousness".

1

Depending on the perspective, the upper or lower row of teeth is visible. First draw the outline of the open mouth. Make sure not to draw it too upright.

2

We can see the upper row of teeth from below. We can only see the lower row of teeth from the front. We can also only slightly see the upper region from the tongue.

3

To make the mouth look more dynamic, you can hatch the throat. Make sure that the lines are parallel to each other and point in the direction in which the mouth is open.

4

When the mouth is pulled apart so strongly, indentations form in the cheek at the side of the mouth. These indentations are indicated by lines parallel to the mouth. Shading is present by default on the back rows of teeth, the tongue and under the lower lip.

OH YES!!!

The neck connects the head with the body. This connection is incredibly important for the expressiveness of the character. Is the neck thin and sloping, or is the neck very wide and stiff?

To have the freedom to draw any neck shapes, it is important to study its anatomy.

Drawing hair is one of the favorite topics of my course participants. On the popularity scale of body parts to be drawn, they come in second place, right after eyes. Is it the same for you?

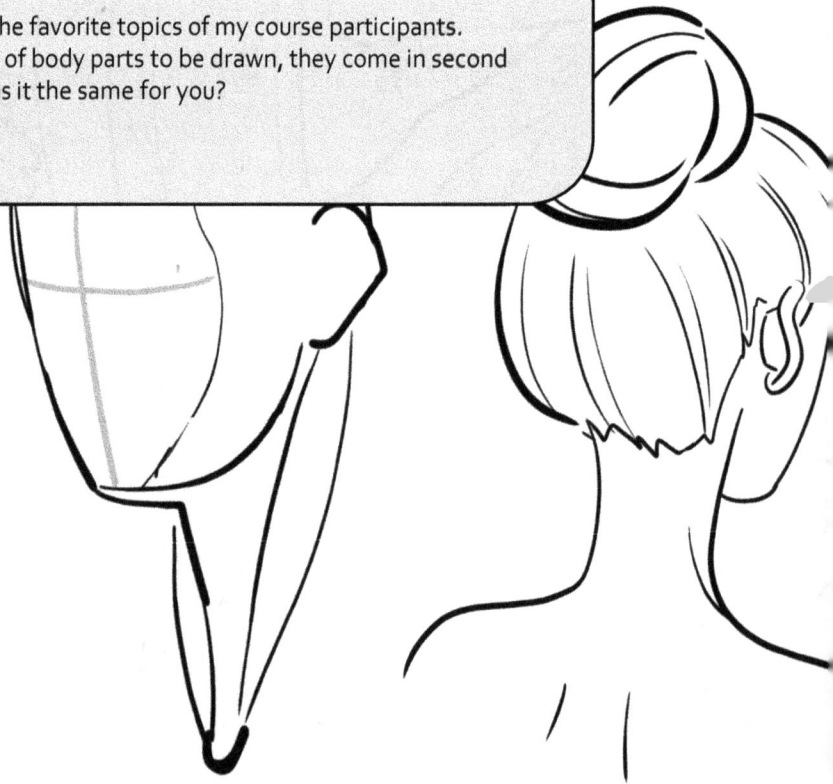

CHAPTER 3

HOW TO DRAW NECK, NAPE & HAIR

3.1 DRAWING THE NECK, NAPE, AND SHOULDERS STEP BY STEP

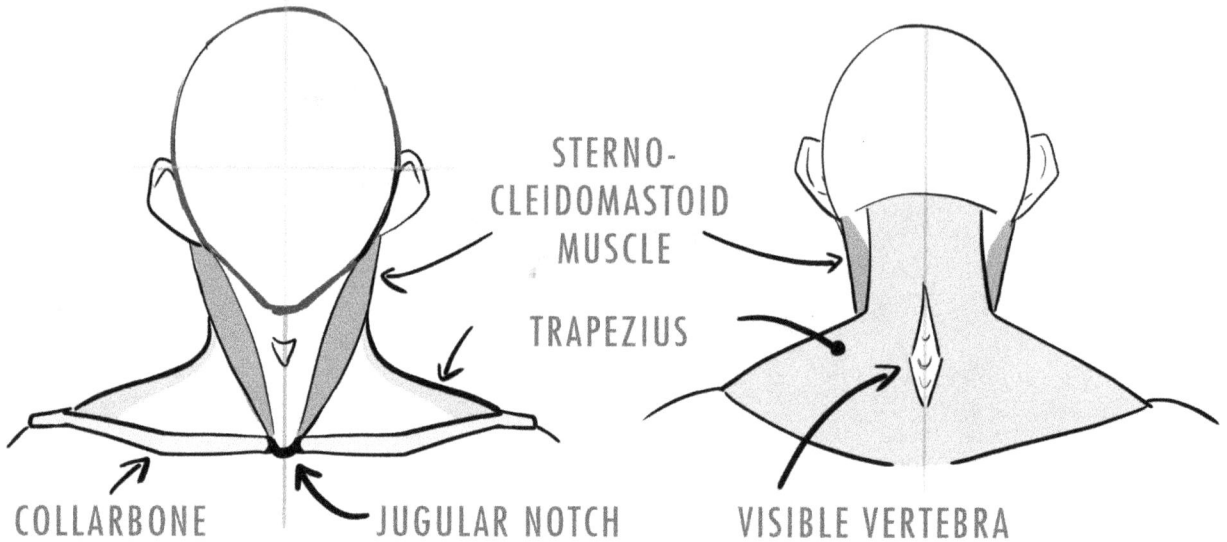

STERNO-
CLEIDOMASTOID
MUSCLE

TRAPEZIUS

COLLARBONE   JUGULAR NOTCH   VISIBLE VERTEBRA

Understanding the anatomy of the neck is not only important when creating muscular characters. This knowledge is also essential for drawing petite figures. Because even though the less stocky characters don't have distinct bulges for the muscles, these are still present, of course. After all, they too must be able to move. With the anatomical knowledge around the neck and shoulder area, you can draw any kind of figure.

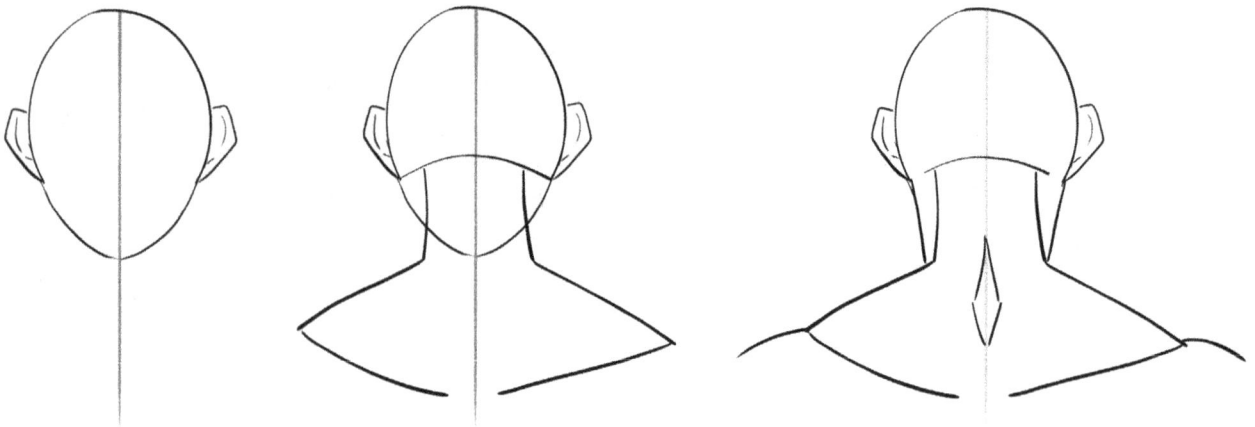

When viewed from behind, you can see in particular the upper trapezius muscle. This muscle lifts the shoulders. Characters who carry heavy weight have a correspondingly strong trapezius muscle. Also visible from this view is the base of the sternocleidomastoid muscle, which starts under the ear and runs forward to the collarbones.

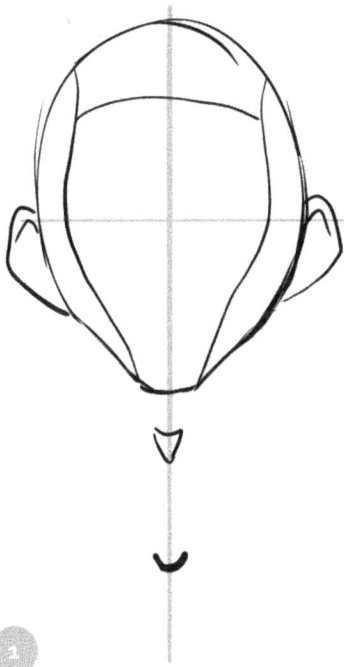

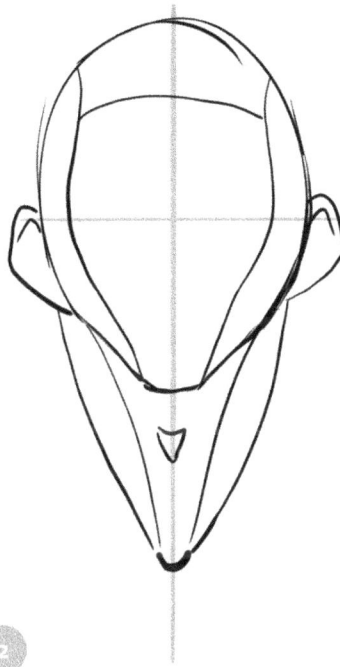

An important orientation point is the jugular, which is the meeting point of the collarbones. This point marks the midline of the neck and chest.
The sternocleidomastoid muscles run towards the jugular notch.
In petite characters, only the base of the sternocleidomastoid muscles can be seen at the jugular notch. In male characters, the larynx can be emphasized by drawing in the shadow it casts.

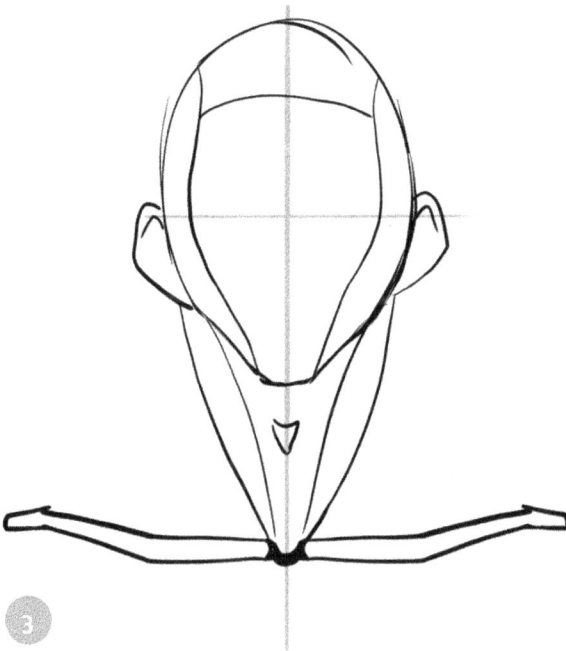

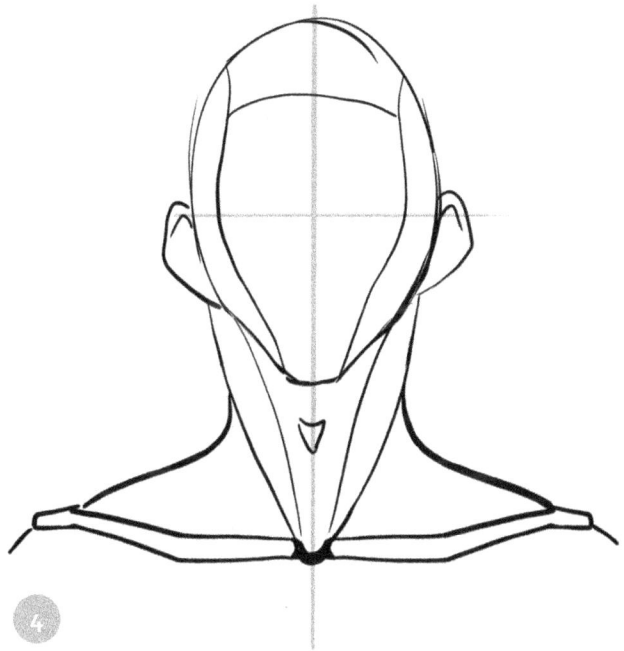

The collarbones originate from the jugular notch. They are rather angular and end between the trapezius muscle and the deltoid muscle of the arms. Feel this area once on yourself. You'll notice a distinct elevation of the collarbone at the top of the shoulder. Of course, you usually don't see the collarbone so clearly, only individual spots stand out. But you should still draw the collarbone completely a couple of times to learn these approaches correctly. The trapezius muscle starts behind the neck and runs to the ends of the collarbones. Pay attention to its shape. As the name implies, it is a muscle. For this reason, the shape is bulged outward, not inward.

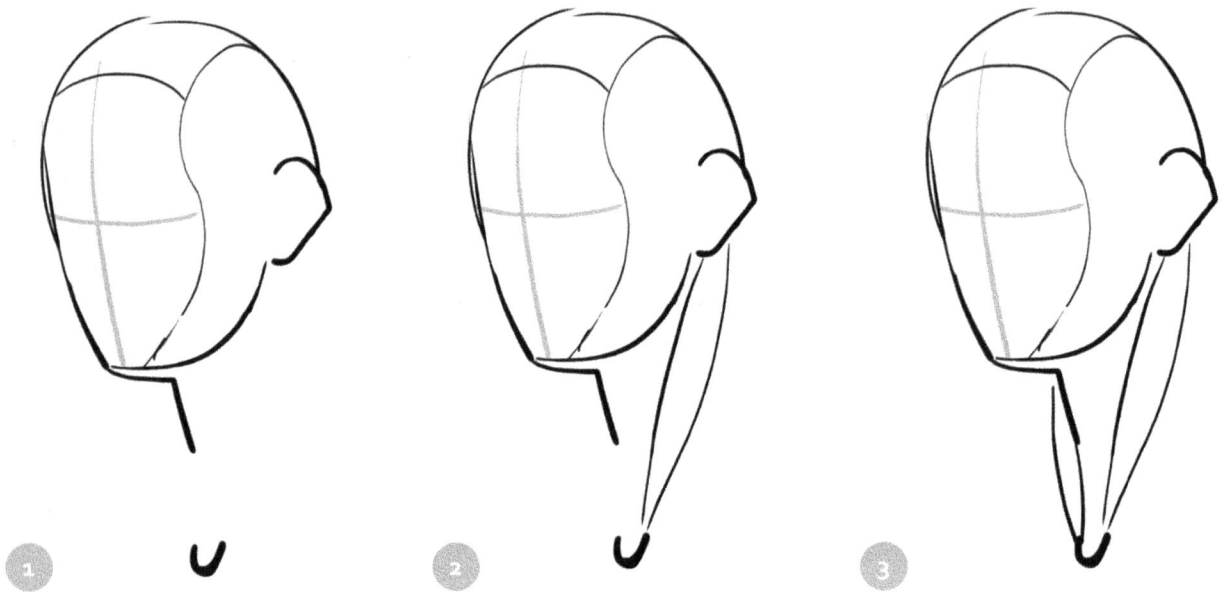

In the 3/4 view, it is also important to find the correct position of the jugular notch. This way, you not only get the position of the neck and the head nodders, but also the perspective approach of the rib cage. This, in combination, provides a good visual balance between the head and the body. The posterior sternocleidomastoid muscle rounds around the neck (trachea) from behind and ends in the jugular notch.

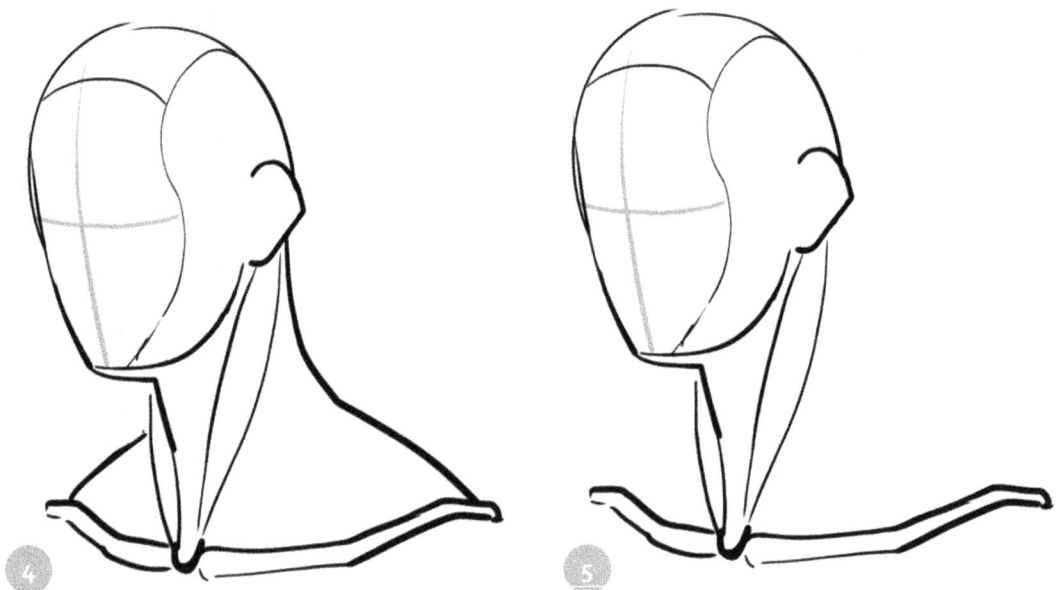

Note the perspective. The posterior shoulder and thus also the posterior collarbone are much more compressed than the right shoulder when viewed from our perspective. At the back shoulder we only see the last bulge of the trapezius muscle.

This bulge is just as high as the bulge on the right shoulder, just not as wide. On the right, the trapezius muscle also runs along the neck.

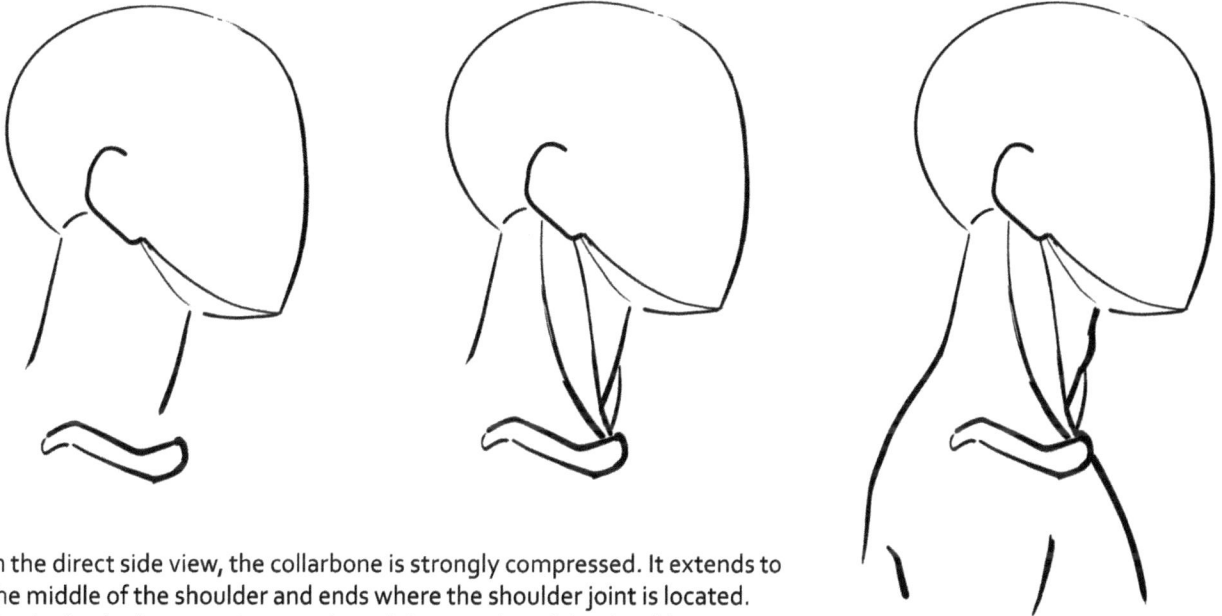

In the direct side view, the collarbone is strongly compressed. It extends to the middle of the shoulder and ends where the shoulder joint is located. On the back, the trapezius muscle and the muscles of the shoulder blade can be seen. In front, the pectoral muscles define the bulge.

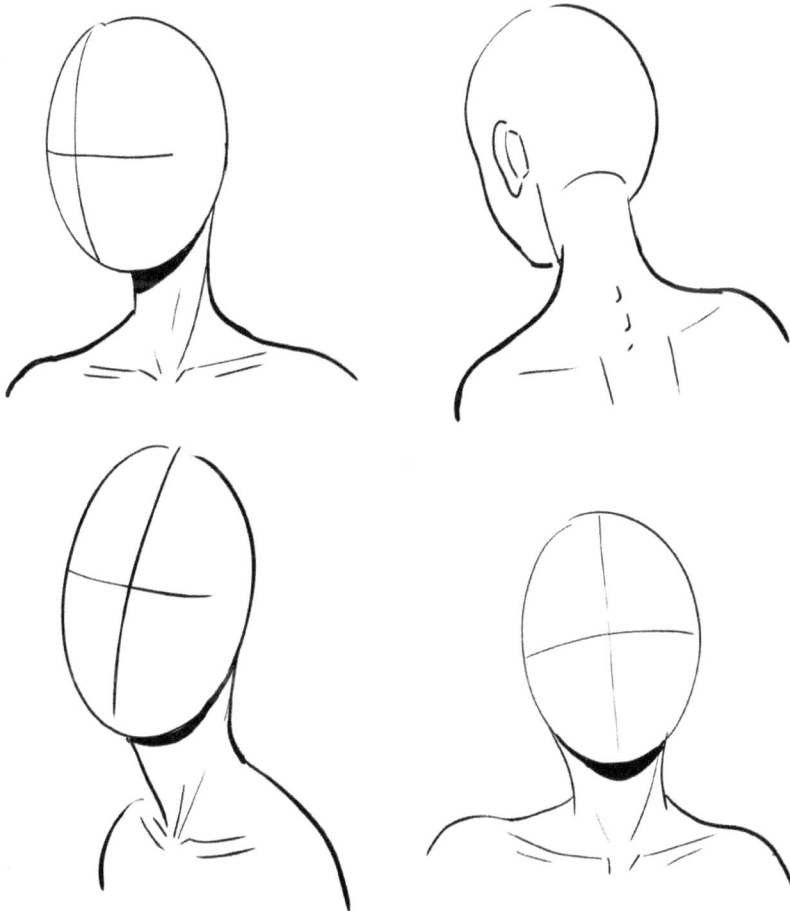

Less muscular figures nevertheless possess visual characteristics of the very anatomy we have learned so far. The clavicles are especially visible at the inner base and in the middle.

The sternocleidomastoid muscles are only visible as slight attachments at the bottom of the collar bones. The trapezius muscle is visible at the outer shoulder line. It is not strongly bulged, but nevertheless present.

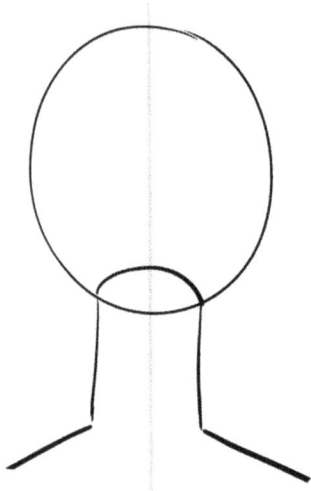
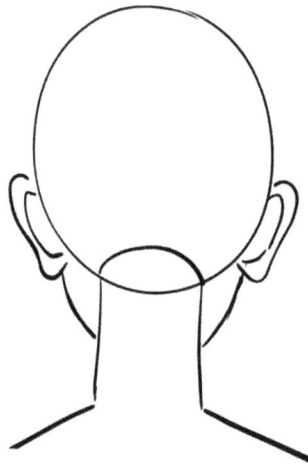
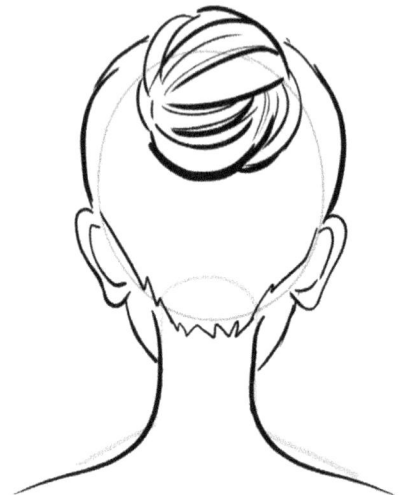

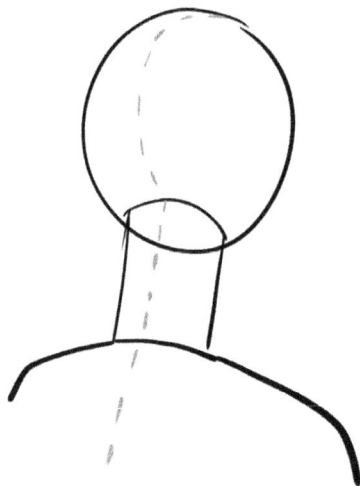
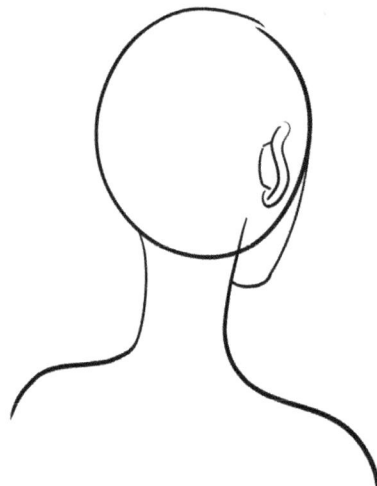

Draw as simplified as possible at the beginning and go through all the steps of this example at your leisure. The view from behind is particularly difficult because there are some small overlaps. The sides of the jaw can be seen well behind the neck and below the ears. The lines of the neck move slightly apart at the top towards the ears. The hair is bound tightly around the round head, so the strands are also rather round. They all run towards the bun.

The earlobe has an S-shape in this perspective. Of course, there are numerous different ear shapes, but this one is quite common.

Notice the fine line that extends from the right shoulder into the neck. This is the course of the upper triceps muscle.

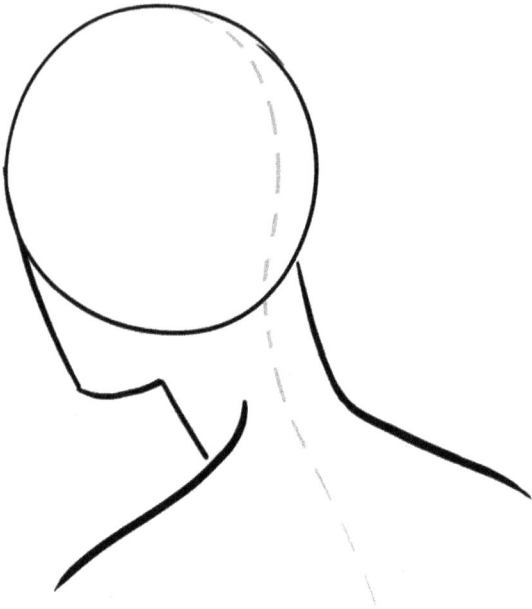

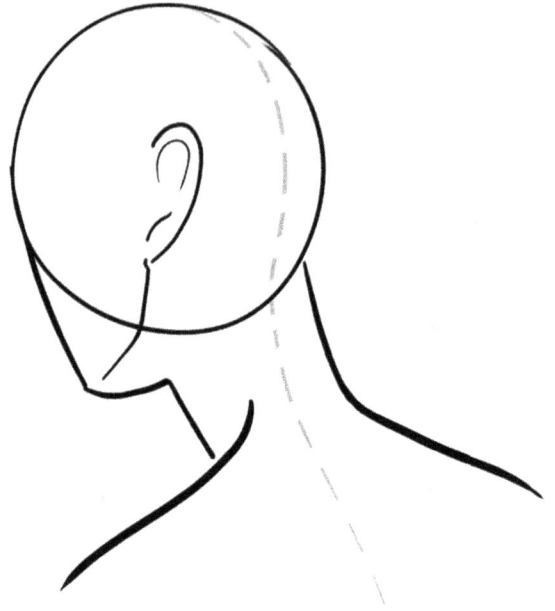

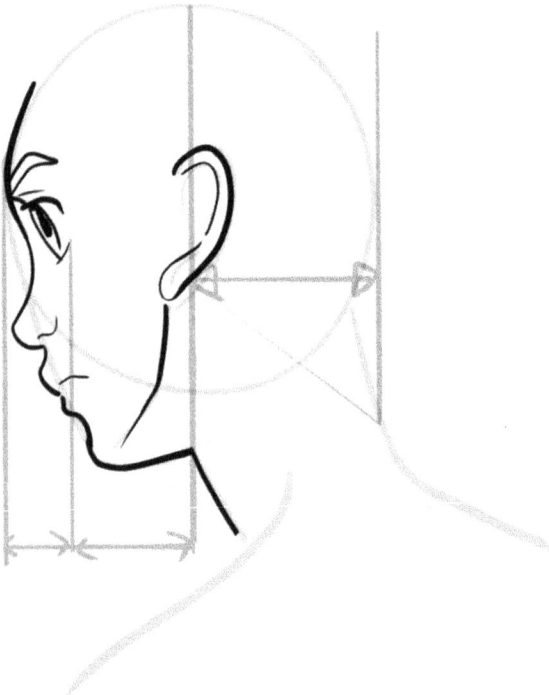

In this view, pay particular attention to the fact that the face is strongly compressed. The back of the head is very present for this. The ear is centered between the back of the head and the face.

3.2 DRAWING HAIR STEP BY STEP

Hair needs lightness and at the same time confidence in the stroke. Finding this balance takes practice. Therefore, feel your way in slowly at first - from stiff hair to lively hairstyles.

First, draw the overall shape of the hair. This can be quite stiff and simplified. You should always start with the basic shape first and only gradually add individual strands.

We now divide the hairstyle into individual strands. These are still quite stiff at first, a little too straight. Make sure that the strands have different sizes. Sometimes a small strand, then a large strand and so on.

Next come the strands and the entire hairstyle of the rounded head shape. The individual strands are still combined into bundles of different sizes. Shading behind the neck and below the strands bring depth to the drawing.

Now you can try your hand at very lively hairs. These hairs stand out more, are more twisted and always have very thin hairs in between.

First, start shading the pony. Draw the strokes from the bottom to the top. The lower area of the pony should be dark and become lighter and lighter towards the top. To do this, first press down hard with the pencil and then reduce the pressure more and more towards the top. Make sure that the hairstyle and thus the strands are rounded.

Then draw in more shading from top to bottom. Leave the light strip free. Draw especially here in the direction in which the hair falls. From top to bottom. The upper part of the hairstyle can be completely dark here. It is important that the lines become thinner and lighter towards the light strip.

Next, I gave the hair more volume by drawing in more thin hairs that break out a little more freely from the hairstyle. I refined the gradient around the light strip. It really takes a lot of strokes, but the result is impressive!

Since I draw digitally, it is no problem to also draw in white, thin hairs afterwards. Make sure that they are really thin. For example, with traditional painting, you could add a few light strands with a white gel pen on top of the black ink drawing. With a pencil drawing, on the other hand, individual highlights can be added by erasing them with a very thin eraser.

For the popular tousled hairstyles, it is helpful to first draw a round border for the hair.

After all, the hair is an extension of the round head. So that you do not deviate too much from this shape, a large circle around the head helps.

Again, make sure that the strand blocks are of different sizes and not too straight.

Draw additional thin strands between the larger strand of hair. The lines of the strand are slightly thicker on the lower sides. This applies especially to the place where the hair falls over the forehead and cast shadows on it.

A simple gradient of hair darkness quickly gives the hairstyle depth and liveliness.

Now take either the same character or draw no face at all and try to collect a number of different hairstyles. Drawing as many different hairstyles as possible is a perfect exercise. This way, you'll expand your possibilities to draw your own characters with great hairstyles.

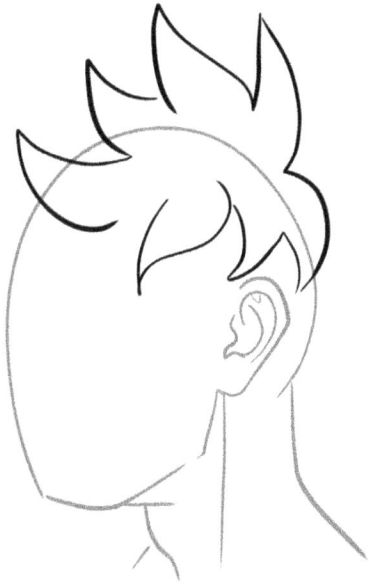

1

A good exercise to achieve a certain ease in tousled hairstyles is to draw many vivid hair bunches. Start with the front row.

2

The second row is behind the first row and has slightly smaller strands. Make sure that the lines of the tousled layers do not meet. This is how you get depth in the hairstyle.

3

Draw a third layer of tousled hair. This has smaller strands and is located at the very back of the head. Add individual strands to the hair. This will make the hairstyle even fluffier.

4

To take the hair to another level, draw in strand divisions with very thin lines. This gives the hairstyle more texture and looks much more detailed. It's rare to draw this detailed in a manga, but it's great for practice!

The longer the hair, the more twists they have. This can become quite complex and opaque. Therefore, start with simple strands that look like longer strips of paper.

Gradually continue to divide these strips of paper.

With longer hair in the wind, you can practice the "twistiness" of the hair especially well. It is important here that you know the starting point of the hair. The hair logically starts at the hairline. However, this can be very different depending on the hairstyle.

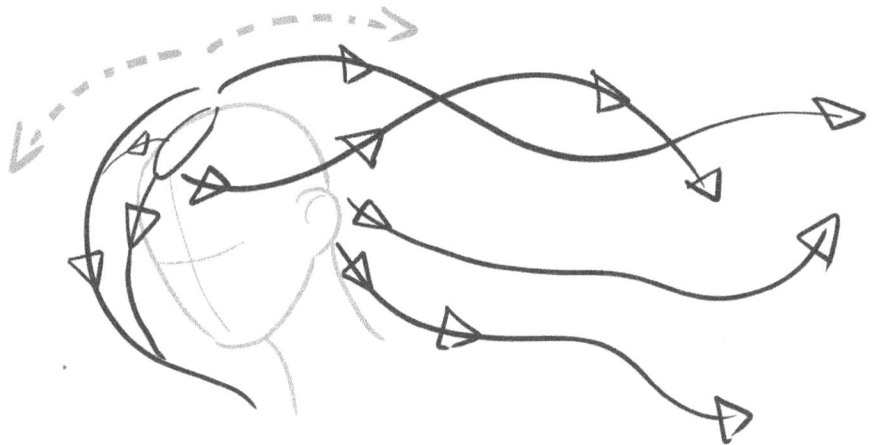

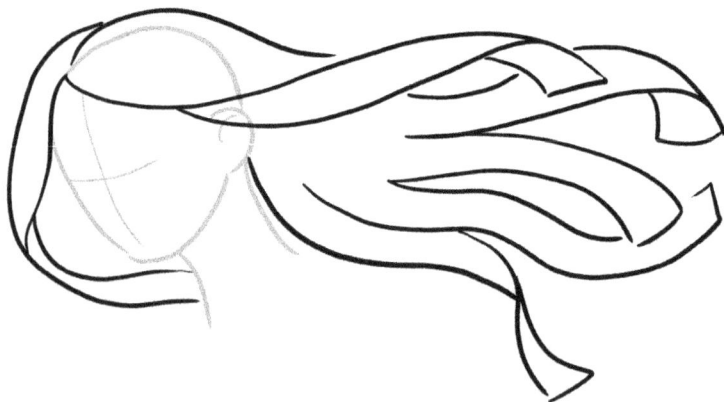

Until you get a feel for hairstyles, it takes some practice. Hair doesn't just fly around wildly, but sometimes it forms clusters, sometimes it's alone, sometimes it moves in one direction or another. For this, look at real photos or videos and try to recognize the structure behind the hair and reproduce it in a simplified way.

Once I am happy with the rough division of the strands, I start to divide the ends of the strands. These remind a little of hands ... The large strands still have quite thick border lines, while the details within these strand clusters are drawn with thin line. After all, we do not want to lose our basic structure.

Additional finer division of the strands plus single strands of hair bring more liveliness to the hairstyle. The strand lines are continuous and often start at the hairline. Try to draw the strand lines cleanly and continuously, not dashed!

In the final step, I give the hair a base color. Highlights on the hair give the hairstyle a final touch. The highlights are always where the hair makes a curve upwards. These areas are at a better angle to the light and thus appear brighter.

A good exercise to learn how to draw more complex hairstyles can be to create monochrome hairstyle outlines. If this outline looks good, you can then work out the individual hair strands.

When drawing hair, it's important not to think about individual strands, but to focus on the entirety of the hairstyle.

This short hairstyle consists of three main parts. The bangs, the side hair that disappears behind the ear and the back hair that falls down. This is seen not only in the different direction of the strands, but also in the different areas of light on the hair. These are caused by the different angles of light reflection.

In this long hairstyle, the very thin strands at the bottom do very well. A slight gradient in the hair darkness quickly gives the whole character a lot of depth. The hair is lighter at the top and gets darker towards the bottom. Whether you draw digitally or traditionally: Build gradients into your drawings. This will improve the result immensely and make your characters look more alive.

In this drawing, pay special attention to where the hair starts and in which direction it runs. An important point of tension in the hair is where the scrunchie presses the hair together.

All hair starting at the head and not belonging to the bangs runs towards the hair tie. From the hair tie, you can restart and draw the hair strands down. The light comes from above, so the lower parts of the hair are in shadow.

3.3 DRAWING BEARD STEP BY STEP

The shape of the beard always reminds me of a meadow when I draw it. Leaves of grass look very similar to beard hairs in manga. Drawing a meadow is also a great exercise and helps you immensely to bring looseness and variety to your stroke. The blades of grass lean in different directions and have different sizes and stroke widths.

 Like a small piece of meadow, the beard has a certain basic shape. You can therefore start the drawing as a triangle, an oval or a rectangle, for example. The individual stubbles are then drawn along this basic shape. Notice how these stubbles resemble blades of grass.

But do not underestimate the drawing of stubbles. It takes a lot of practice and looseness in the wrist. In the beginning, you may therefore draw rather stiff, lifeless strokes.

Gradually try to make your movements more fluid and uncontrolled. As soon as you have drawn a full meadow with blades of grass, you will automatically become looser. And eventually you won't even think about each blade of grass or stubble. Instead, your hand will begin to move on its own.

The hairline plays a significant role in drawing - both hairstyles and beards. Not only does the hair start here, the hairline is also the transition between hair and skin. Always draw the transition as thin as possible, preferably even with small interruptions. This way it looks less like the character is wearing a glued-on wig.

You can make the lines thicker where the beard ends. At the base, however, your lines should remain rather thin.

Sometimes it's difficult to find the correct hairline directly. However, it is super important for your drawing. So be sure to draw it in before you give your character a beard. That way, you'll always know where the beard goes. The beard will keep its symmetry and the drawing will look more coherent overall.

The hair at the hairline is finer and less lively compared to the outer beard hair and the rest of the hairstyle. Note that the chin determines the shape of the beard. Try to enhance the character of the chin with the help of the beard.

IMPORTANT TIP:

For step by step instructions on how to draw this grandpa without a beard, see the chapter "Drawing older people"

Now try to draw these different beard shapes first. Note that the base of the beard has a fairly thin line. The lateral lines and the lower line of the beard, on the other hand, are comparatively thick. It often happens that the mouth is covered by the beard and is barely visible. In these cases, it is still important to at least hint at the position of the mouth. You achieve this by a slightly dashed area. Also think about slighty indicating the lower lip. There are no facial hair on the lip itself, but the beard often starts under the lower lip.

Practice and research are also important when it comes to beards. Look for pictures of real beards and try to simplify them. If you still have difficulty drawing a face, do not draw it in completely. An oval for the head shape is enough. Concentrate on drawing the hair of the beard.

All beard shapes shown here are based on real models. First, you should follow such models. Once you have the necessary practice, you can of course also develop your own cool beard shapes.

LEVEL 1 – CHIBI

Especially for beginners, it is a good idea to start drawing in *chibi* style. This does not mean that chibi characters are easy to draw. However, they are simplified at first so that one does not immediately fall into stress.

And even for advanced beginners it can be worthwhile to start with a chibi face as an exercise. This way you can check where you are at.

The important thing is: with every exercise there is something new to learn. So, let's get started!

CHAPTER 4

DRAWING A CHIBI BOY FROM THREE ANGLES

4.1 CHIBI BOY: FRONT VIEW

Symmetry is important when looking from the front. But be careful: Avoid mirroring one half of the face at all costs. This will look unnatural. Nobody's face is completely symmetrical. The halves always show differences. Therefore, draw boldly freehand. It's perfectly okay if not everything is perfectly symmetrical.

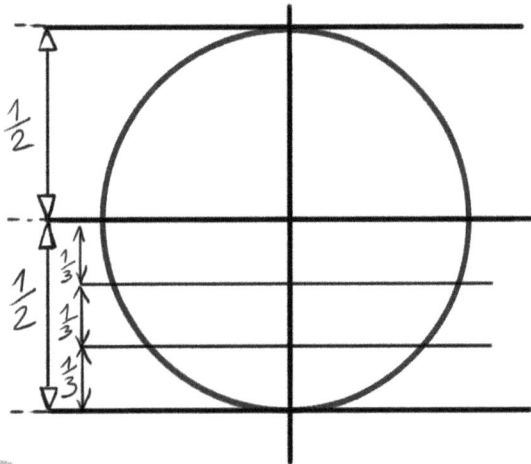

The best way to start a chibi character is always with a circle. Try to practice circles on a scratch sheet. It doesn't have to be a perfect circle, but it should look reasonably symmetrical.

Then draw a vertical and horizontal bisecting line. Divide the bottom half into three more sections.

If you draw digitally, create these guides on a separate layer. This way you can easily hide them later. If you use a pencil, draw these guides very lightly. This will make it easier to erase them later.

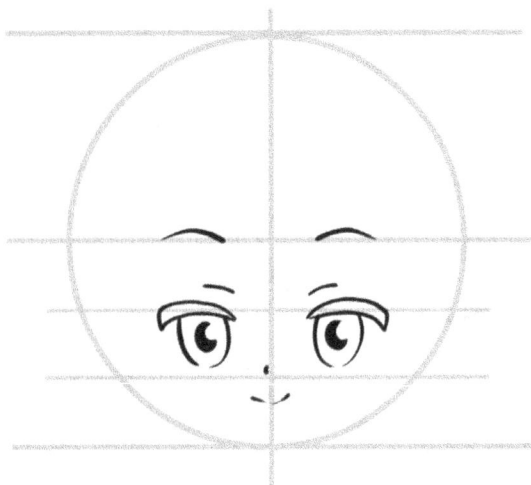

We draw the face in the lower half of the circle. The eyebrows start with a slightly thicker line and become thinner towards the outside.

For the eyes, make sure that another eye would fit between them. Draw the iris and pupil a little more inward. As if your figure were squinting slightly.

Make sure that the nose is just below the eyes or even at the same height as the eyes. In addition, the nose is slightly to the side of the head midline. The mouth is closer to the nose rather than the chin. The mouth line can be interrupted in the middle.

The lower part of the jaw and chin fits exactly the circle line. You can also draw the chin more pointed. However, a round chin makes the character sweeter. The neck is centered, has a cylinder shape, and flares out slightly at the bottom. There the shoulder muscles begin. The outer line of the ears connects super with the line of the jaw.

Note that the jaw with the ears no longer follows the circle line, but is drawn further inside. The inner lines of the ear are best drawn in thinner.

With hair, it is important to know in which direction the strands of hair fall. This is often different, depending on the hairstyle and where the hair is combed.

But of course, they always start at the hairline on the head. In our case, we let them start at the top and fall down along the head.

Hair is an extension of the round head shape, so always make sure to suggest roundness with the hair.

With hair, it is also especially important that they look fluffy and lively.

Therefore, please draw the strand lines thinner on the upper side and thicker on the lower side. Also, make sure to keep a certain level of energy behind the shape. Stay loose and don't draw too stiff!

5

6

7

In order for the drawing to gain depth, we need shadows. We assume that the light comes from above. So the shapes that turn away from the light become darker. The undersides of the hair strands are thus in shadow. The hair strands also create shadows on the face. There are also shadows on the inside of the ear, the drop shadow under the chin on the neck, and the shadow on the eye from the upper eyelid.

These shadows can be painted digitally with the color gray, hatched with pencil or drawn in the colorful variant with dark color.

Finally, I give the hair a darkness and draw the "ring of light" along the head. This ring with interruptions creates once again more liveliness and a certain three-dimensionality.

Digitally, it's very simple: draw a white ring around the hair on a separate layer and then erase individual spots. With a pencil you would have to leave out the light areas.

I hope you had fun with the drawing and learned a few things! :)

4.2 CHIBI BOY: SIDE VIEW

Always remember that these instructions are examples. At first, it's best to draw along step by step and stick to my instructions. But after that, feel free to play around with the proportions and try to draw different characters. People and manga characters are highly individual and everyone has their own unique proportions. Therefore, not all characters can be drawn with the same construction method.

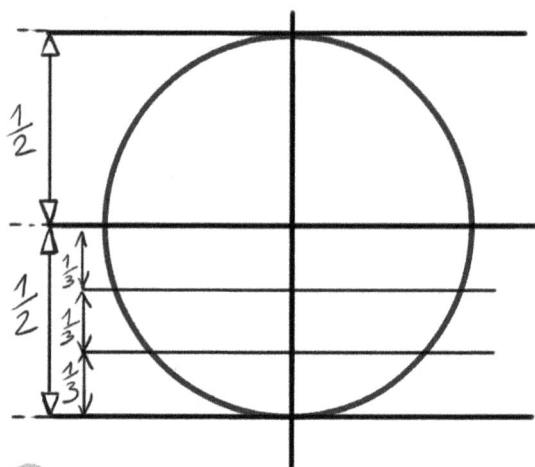

As with the front view, we use very similar construction lines. The proportions also remain the same.

Here, too, don't despair if it doesn't turn out to be a perfect circle. Try to draw the circle not from the wrist, but from the elbow or shoulder. shoulder. This gives you more control over the line.

Keep in mind that the other lines are only guides and we won't need them later.

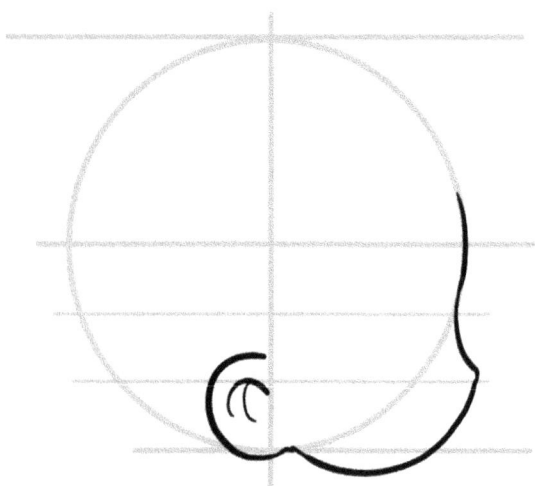

For the side view, I like to start with the face line first. The forehead runs along our circle and the transition to the nose and mouth can be drawn in a shape. The line of the mouth, chin, and jaw ends right at the ear. A beautiful line outlining so many things!

The ear in this case lies against the center line.

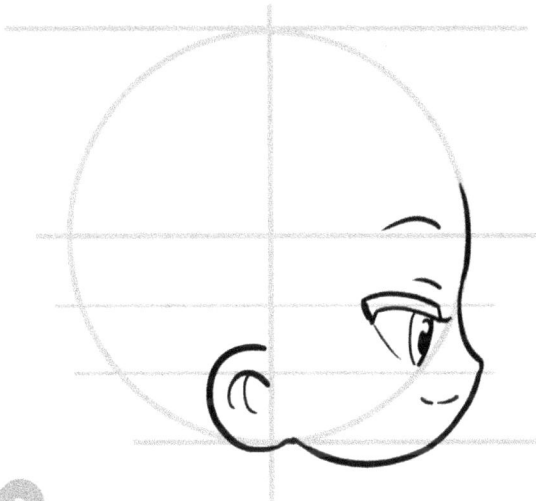

Note with the eyebrow that it has some distance to the brow line. It also lies above the eye and parallel to it.

The eye itself has a triangular shape when viewed from the side. Where the pupil is located, the eye is rounded. Finally, the eye is a sphere. The iris and the pupil are strongly curved. They are no longer circles, but ellipses.

Draw the mouth further up. It is closer to the nose rather than the chin.

At this point, I found it fitting to add the character's shoulders. At the same time, this is a great exercise! Note here that the neck is slightly tilted. No one stands bolt upright all the time. From the neck, the chest starts off on the right and the shoulder muscles and shoulder blades are on the left.

The sleeve has a little distance from the collar. With it we indicate the width of the shoulder.

The hair "flows" from the hairline. Imagine the strands full of dynamic, then draw the hair not too stiff.

6

7

8

When shading, I make sure that shapes that stick out also cast shadows. The strands of hair, for example, or even the ear and the head, which casts a shadow on the neck. A larger shadow on the hair at the back of the head brings more roundness to the head as a whole.

As before, the light ring has interruptions again and again. These interruptions give the strands additional volume. This effect is enhanced when the white ring has some distance from the outer line of the hair.

We can also place two light spots on the strands at the very top of the head. This also gives them more three-dimensionality.

4.3 CHIBI-BOY: ¾ VIEW

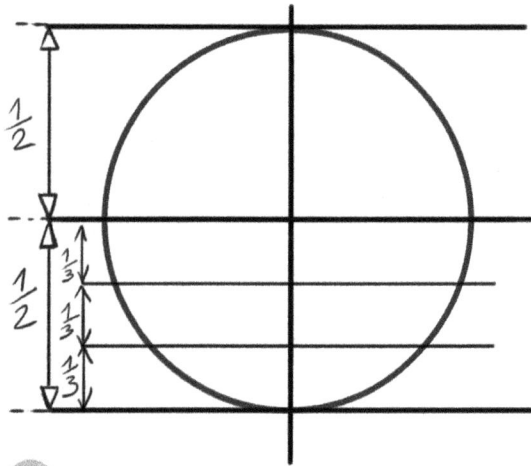

$\frac{1}{2}$

$\frac{1}{2}$

$\frac{1}{3}$

$\frac{1}{3}$

$\frac{1}{3}$

The round head shape remains the same in the ¾ view. This also applies to the most important proportions. So we can use the identical guides here as well.

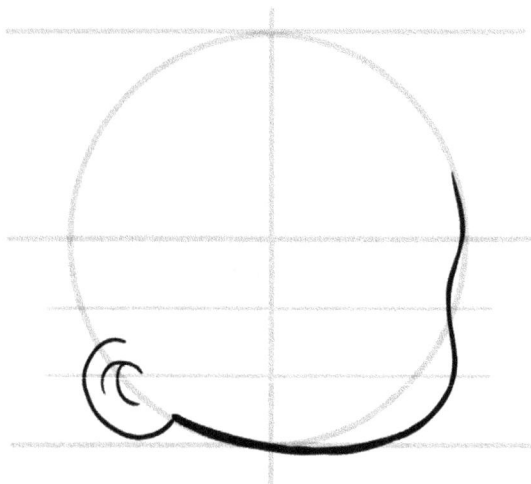

To define the lower part of the face, one line is enough. This starts above the center line at the circle. The forehead initially runs along the circle. There is an indentation in the area of the eyes. This is followed by a bulge for the back of the cheek.

Across the cheek, the chin and jaw line runs fairly smoothly to the ear. In this case, the ear itself is relatively far down and somewhat more oblique. Use the circle as a guide here as well. This will help you with the alignment.

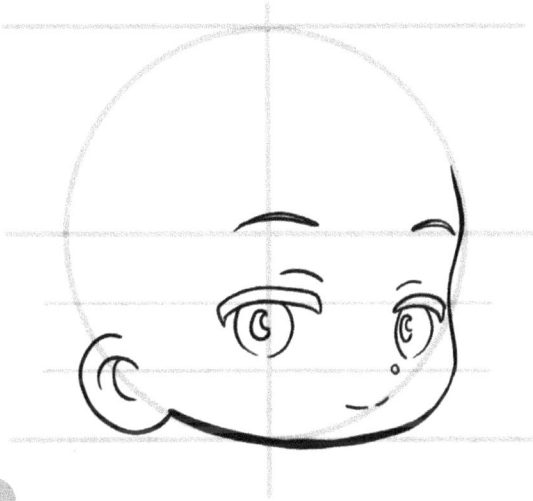

We have already drawn the face from the front. Here we now have a perspective, in this case a view diagonally from the side. Everything away from us, in particular the back half of the face, is now compressed.

The left eyebrow and the left eye as seen from us are barely distorted. They look quite similar to the front view. You can use the vertical center line as a guide for the placement of the left eye.

The back half of the face, on the other hand, is clearly compressed. The nose is close to the back eye.

The eyebrows and the eyes are at the same height. However, the back eye has only half the width. The iris and the pupil are also compressed. They are no longer circles, but ellipses.

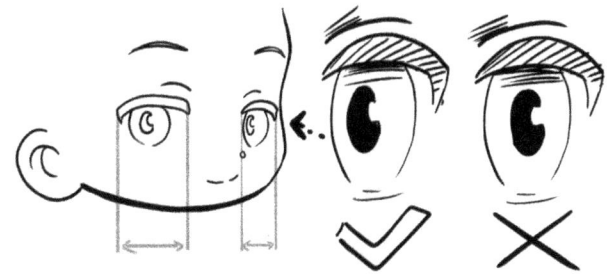

The back eyebrow is also strongly compressed. Also note that the pupil of the back eye is positioned more on the left edge of the iris. This way, the eye looks more to the left away from us, instead of directly straight ahead.

When drawing the neck, you can again use the center line as a great guide. It lies under the left eye, has a cylindrical shape and is slanted.

The collar rounds around the neck.

5

6

7

By the way: You are welcome to color or shade my finished outline drawings.

Try it out!

LEVEL 2 – SHOJO

Next we draw a girl in the typical *shojo* style.

Again, the head is based on a circle. However, the chin and the individual facial components are worked out in greater detail than we saw with the chibi boy.

The *shojo* style is characterized by large eyes, a small nose and a fine mouth. The eyebrows are thin and lie well above the eyes. The forehead is often very high, which gives the characters their particular cuteness.

CHAPTER 5

DRAWING A SHOJO GIRL DRAW FROM THREE ANGLES

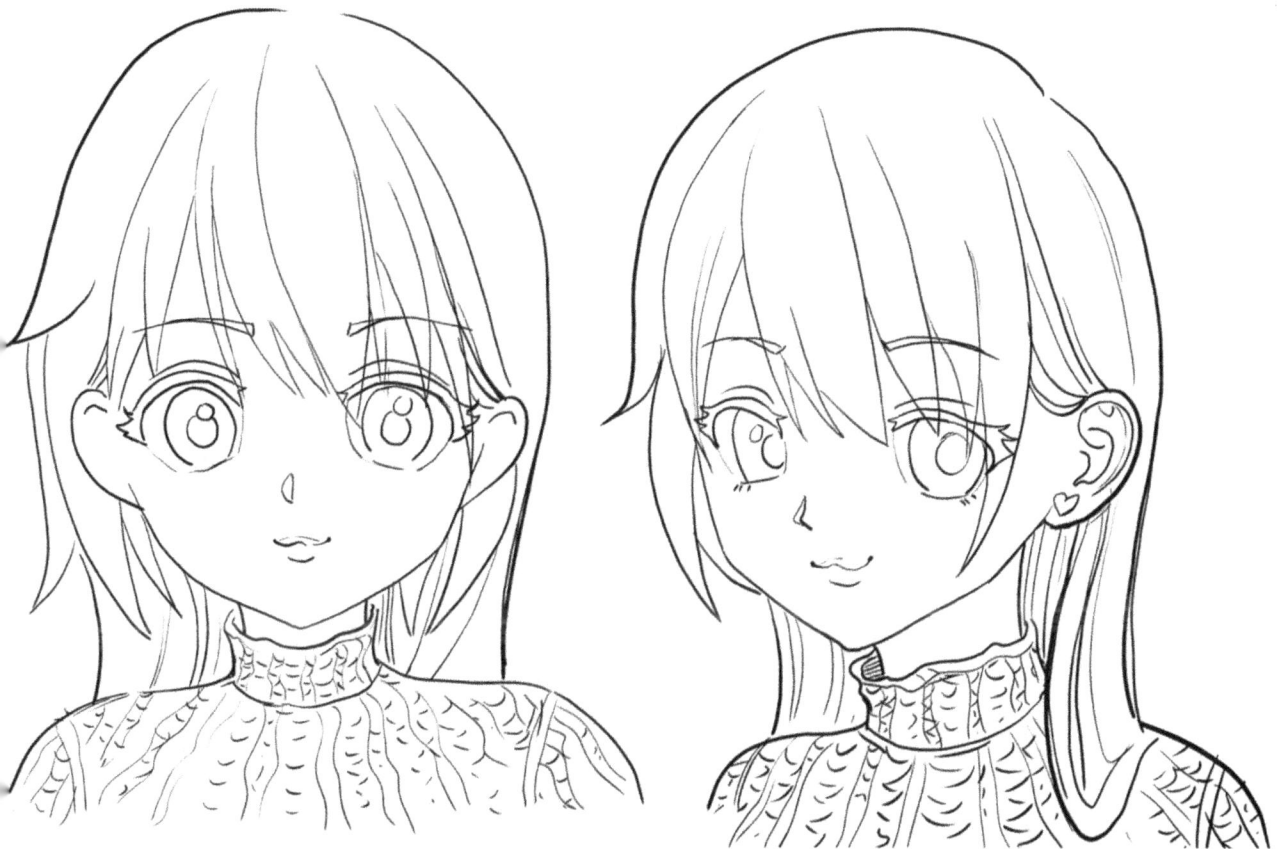

5.1 SHOJO GIRL: FRONT VIEW

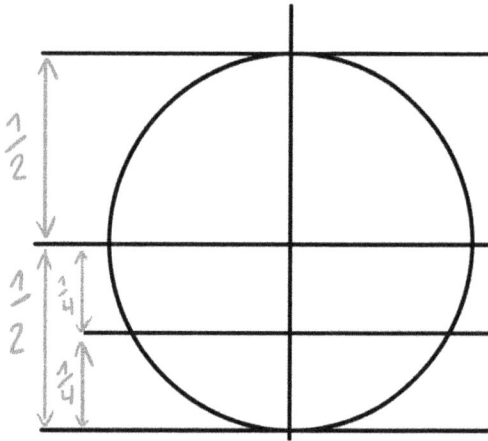

Compared to the chibi style, the use of the circle changes somewhat. The chin is no longer at the bottom of the circle, but is drawn below it (to be seen later).

For the lower half of the circle, the division into halves is enough for us this time.

On the other hand, we actually always need the horizontal and vertical bisecting line. Even professional portrait artists use center lines to guide them.

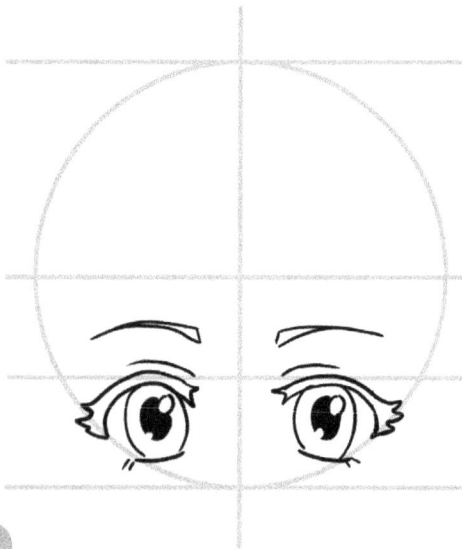

We start with the eyes. Avoid drawing one eye and just copying the second – especially if you draw digitally.

Symmetry is important. But don't overdo it, or the character will quickly resemble a cyborg. So rather erase as needed and try to achieve symmetry little by little.

First draw the left eye and then the right eye.

For detailed step-by-step instructions, see the eyes chapter.

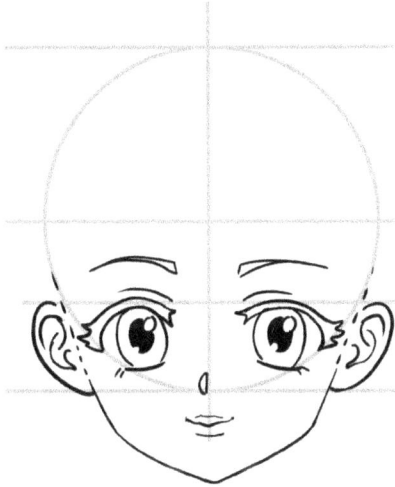

Now, we add the chin and jaw line. This line connects to the circle. How much chin you draw depends on what age and character you want to give your character. In this case, I chose about the height of a quarter of the bottom circle area.

I position the ears at about the same height as the eyes. The nose is slightly next to the vertical center line at the height of the lower eyelids.

For the mouth, the middle line (between the upper and lower lips) is most important. Note that the thin lines for the upper and lower lip do not touch this middle line.

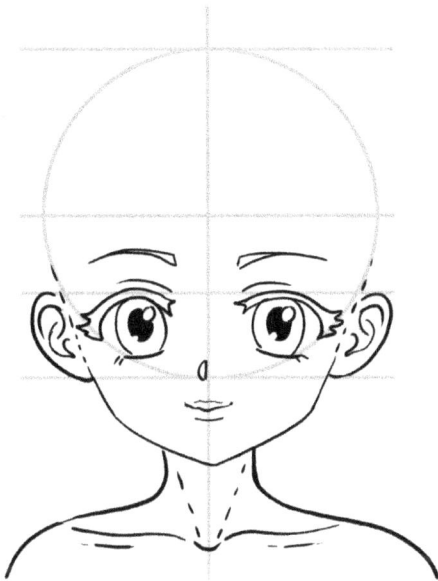

Before you draw in the shoulders with clothes, try to remember the anatomy of the neck and shoulders (Chapter 3.1). At the bottom of the middle of the neck is the jugular notch. This is where the two collarbones meet. In addition, the two sternocleidomastoid muscles, which run behind the ear, are also located there.

When we draw in the clothes, we can still see the choke pit, the upper side of the collarbones and a slight approach of a sternocleidomastoid muscle. Be careful, however, that the figure doesn't look too lean. Also note that the clothes are over the body and have some distance from it.

Let's continue with the hair!

6

7

8

Do not draw the hair as individual highlights, but draw groups of highlights. These are sometimes larger and sometimes smaller.

Be careful not to draw the hair too parallel. Hair is difficult to control in reality.

The lines of the hair should therefore be lively. This means that you use different stroke widths for the lines and that some strands break out of the shape a bit. I drew the outer line of the hair a little thicker, while the strands inside have slightly thinner lines. This way the hair becomes one unit.

9

10

11

The most important places for shading are behind the neck by the back hairs. This gives the drawing much more depth. Also important is the shading in the front by the strands. This gives the head a rounded three-dimensionality.

Shading under the chin, nose, upper lip and upper eyelid also create further depth and vibrancy. Now it only remains for us to color in the hair and clothing. The light streak on the hair should be slightly rounded. With the black strand lines are the typical interruptions.

5.2 SHOJO GIRL: SIDE VIEW

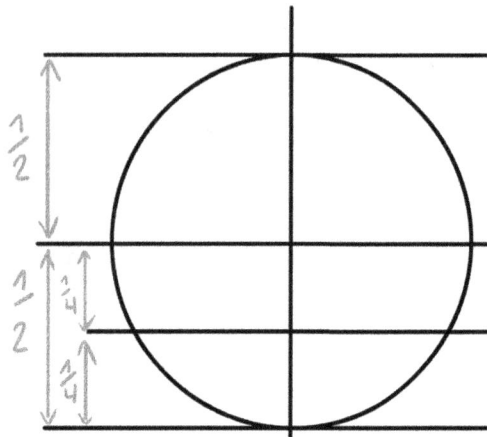

As with the front view, we use very similar construction lines. The proportions remain the same.

Again, don't despair if it doesn't turn out to be a perfect circle. Try to draw the circle not from the wrist, but from the elbow or shoulder. This way you have more control over the line.

Keep in mind that these are only guide lines and we won't need them later.

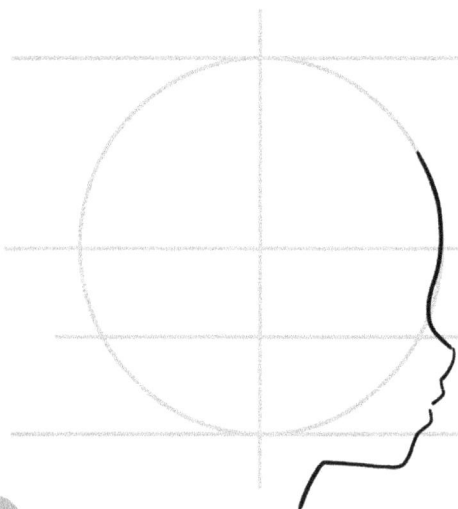

For the side view, I prefer to start with the face line. The forehead runs along our circle and the transition to the nose and mouth can be drawn in a shape. The line of the mouth, chin, and jaw ends right at the ear. As you already know, I especially like this line!

In this case, the ear lies against the center line.

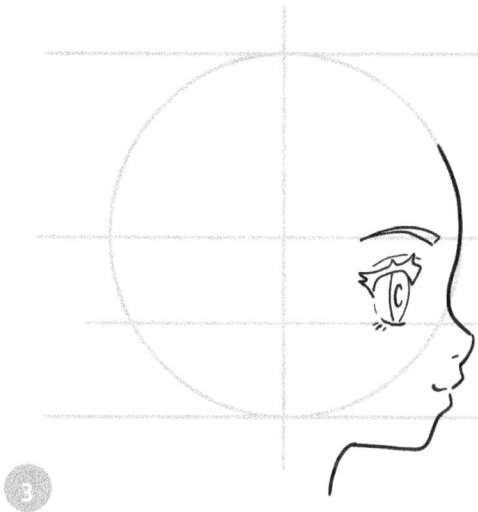

Note with the eyebrow that it has some distance to the brow line. It also lies above the eye and parallel to the upper eyelid.

The eye, iris and pupil are quite compressed. There remains a certain roundness, but just a very compressed one.

We draw the eyelashes not as thin strokes, but as rough bundles. Here, we can draw only the outlines for now and color them later. The nostril and smiling mouth are lightly indicated.

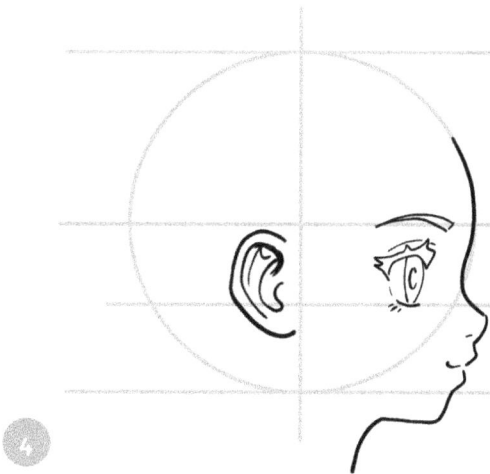

We can align the ear with the center of our construction circle. Draw it at a slight angle and about the same height as the eye and nose.

Draw the ear in as much detail as possible, this is a good exercise (see the chapter: "Drawing the ear). In this example, the ear is quite large so I can draw in the details better. Besides, it fits well with this figure.

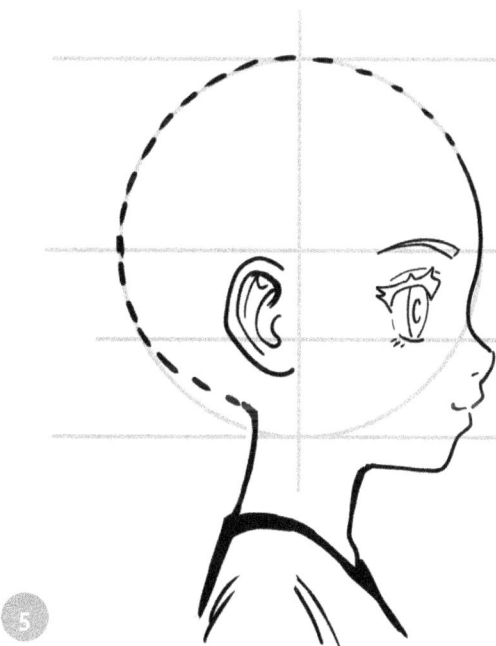

We can conveniently use the circle as a skull line. Note, however, that the skull deviates slightly from the circular shape at the base of the neck. The neck is slanted.

The back line goes slightly outward. The thoracic line goes more outward. There is a small mound between the neck and the chest line for the collarbones.

92

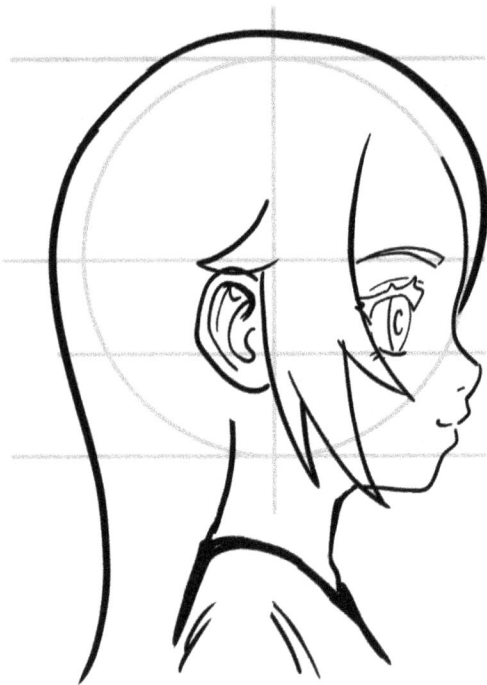

6

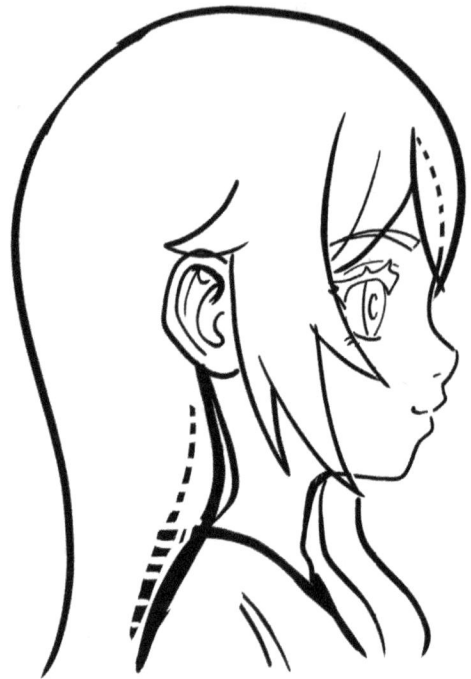

7

8

In the upper part, the hair rests against the skull of our circle construction. That is why the line is very round. The hair follows the shape of the skull.

On the way down, the outer hair line on the left keeps a distance from the neck and shoulders.

The part of the hair that starts at the ear and "snakes" from there over the shoulders is a bit more difficult to draw. This is because at this point the hair overlaps part of the neck and shoulders.

From the ear, the hair first falls relatively straight down. However, they compress as soon as they meet the shoulders. Then they follow the shape of the shoulder and then the back.

Make sure that the neck does not become too thin.

The shading runs along the larger strand bundles. Where the hair lies over the body, shadow is also created. There is also a large area of shadow under the side strand of hair and the jaw.

The light streak starts a bit thicker this time and gets thinner towards the front. This fits the figure well and makes her head rounder.

5.3 SHOJO GIRL: VIEW ¾

The 3/4 view is already a face in perspective. Here, the back half of the face is compressed and shortened. When drawing in perspective, one of the important things is to think threedimensionally. Think of the face you're drawing not as a flat 2D shape, but as an object with volume and depth. For example, it helped me to make a manga head in clay or to develop a 3D model in a computer program.

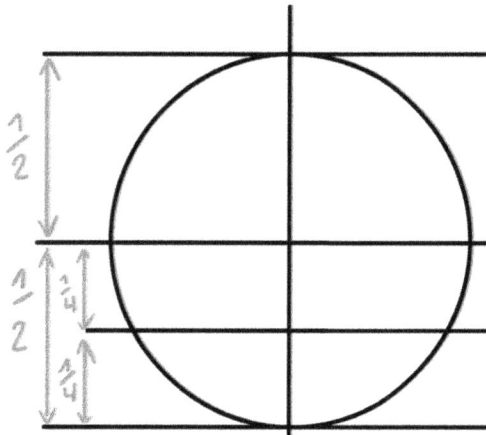

Since this is also the same shojo character as before, we use the identical construction lines.

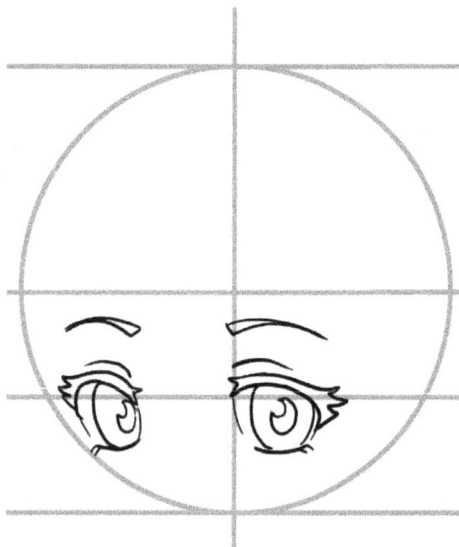

In this perspective, it is important to note that the eyes and eyebrows are still the same height. The pupils, the highlights and the eyebrows are on the same horizontal line. Finally, perspective does not take place in height, but in width.

However, the back eye and the back eyebrow are almost half as wide compared to the front eye. In addition, both eyes are rather shifted to the left and thus very close to the left edge of the circle.

A good reference point for the right eye and eyebrow is the vertical center line of the circle.

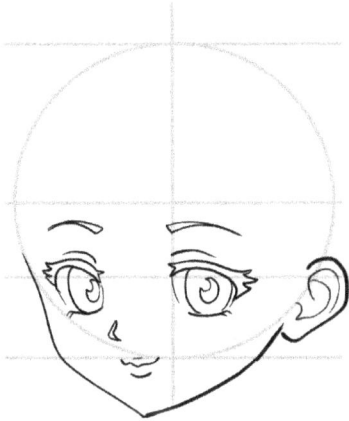

The jaw-chin line starts at the circle. At the same time, the line has a certain angularity. It is no longer simply round like in the chibi style. Here, the chin is relatively pointed and is to the left of the vertical midline of the face.

The nose is close to the back of the eye. The shape of the nose bulges out to the left.

The left corner of the mouth is below the nose.
The entire mouth is between the two eyes, positioned slightly closer to the right eye. Do not draw the mouth too deep.

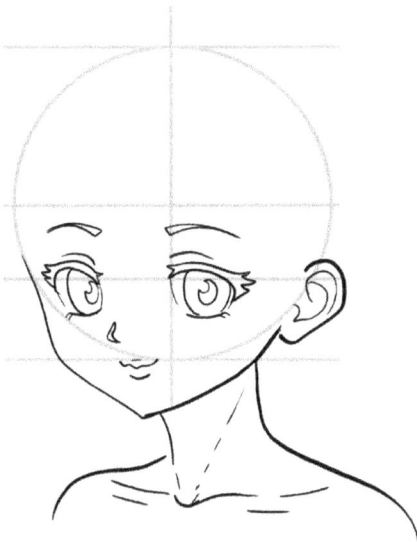

You can first draw in the neck and shoulder area without the clothing. An important point here is the jugular notch. As you know, this is where the two collarbones meet. The jugular notch defines the center of the chest area. The back (left) shoulder is narrower than the front shoulder because of the depth.

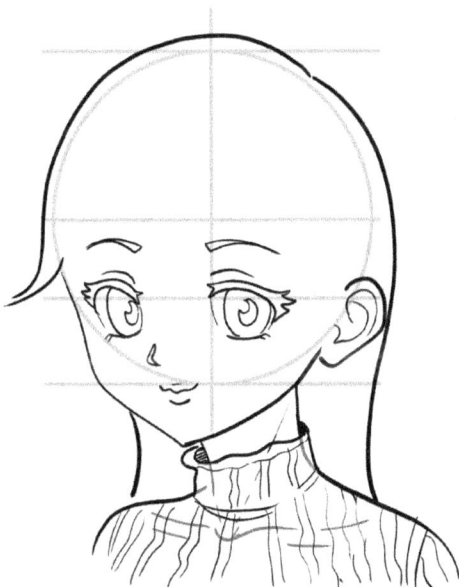

Draw the sweater with a little distance from the body, especially at the collar. The garment is an extension of the body and rests against the body. At another point, in turn, it protrudes further.

Now we can start with the hair and first draw the outer hair line.

To make a drawing look more impressive, it is recommended to draw the hair more energetically. Imagine that the wind would move the hair a little, or that the figure would have a certain aura that would keep the hair somewhat on hold.

To achieve this effect, I often draw protruding hair and try to make the lower part of the hairstyle particularly expansive. As if the hair was flying apart behind the girl's back.

Behind the neck, I draw many strands with thin line. Behind the ear, the hair piles up. I emphasize this with a dark spot. The outer hair line (just like the outer clothing line) I keep a little thicker. The inner lines, on the other hand, are thinner.

(9)

(10)

Again, the main shading is between the neck and hair, under the chin, under the upper eyelids, between the strands, under the strands and on the lower sides of the strands.

Other additional light shadows come into play at the upper lip, along the jaw, around the pupils, at the ear and on her sweater.

The light strip runs around the hair and starts a little thicker on the left. Sometimes it looks better if the light strip is a little more uneven.

Note that the light strip has interruptions on the hair - where the borders of the strands run.

LEVEL 3 – SHONEN

Now let's move on to a more adult and detailed drawing style. It is still a typical manga style, which could be classified in the shonen area. However, the difficulty level is a bit higher, making the drawing more challenging.

The character is still "cute", but not as extremely cute as the previous examples. The eyes and forehead are smaller in this style relative to the rest of the face.

The eyes, nose, chin and hair are also drawn with more detail. Anatomical knowledge is now becoming more important and practicing individual facial features more indispensable.

CHAPTER 6

SHONEN BOY
STEP BY STEP

$\frac{1}{2}$

$\frac{1}{2}$

6.1 SHONEN BOY: ¾ VIEW

The circle can also be chosen as the starting point here. However, a clear piece of jaw is added. The length of the jaw and chin make the character look more adult. In the chibi and shojo characters, the chin or jaw were barely pronounced, if at all.

The neck connects the shoulders to the head at a slightly oblique angle. We do not want to draw a stiff character. The neck has a cylindrical shape.

The shape of the shoulders connects to the neck. Think of it like a kit that interlocks. Draw in important proportions and ratios as needed. Also compare the position of the head to the neck and shoulders.

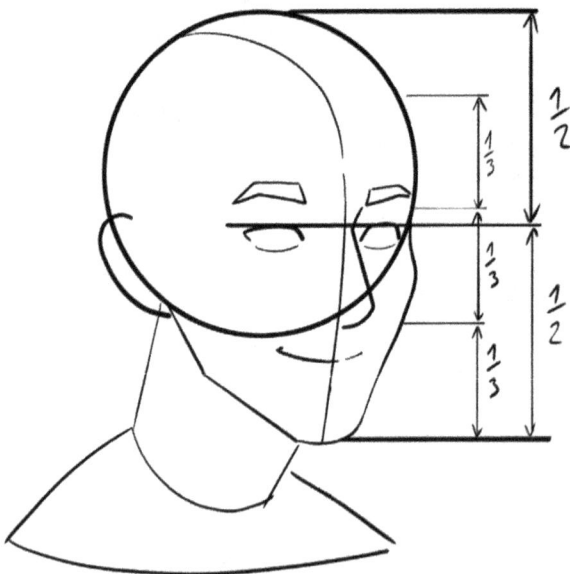

The eyes are slightly below the bisecting line between the chin and the top of the head. The distance from the hairline to the eyebrows, the distance from the eyebrows to the tip of the nose, and the distance between the nose and the chin are approximately the same.

Please note that these are approximate distances. Feel free to measure from time to time, but it doesn't have to be to the millimeter. It is more important that you train your drawing eye. This way, you will be able to estimate the distances more and more with your eye.

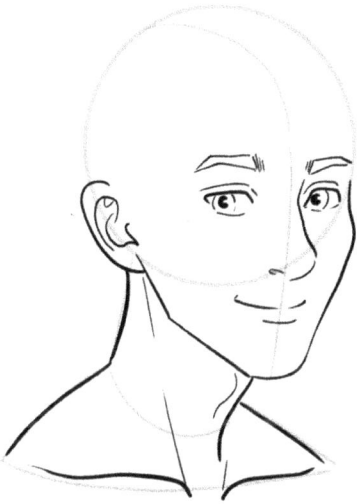

One more note about the vertical midline on the face: this runs from the center of the chin to the center between the eyebrows and then continues roundly across the forehead and the top of the head.

When the basic shapes and proportions fit, I work in the anatomy and details.
"But why shouldn't I just draw correctly right away?" you may be asking yourself.
Because the simplified basic shapes help you focus solely on the proportions.

After that, you can fully devote yourself to the vividness of the lines without having to worry too much about the proportions at the same time.

A step-by-step approach is extremely important when learning.
Even advanced drafters will benefit from this approach and create cleaner and more accurate drawings.

The hairstyle of this figure is a bit more complex. However, if you proceed step by step and draw in the basic shape first, this head full of hair will also be easy to create.

There are some overlays in this hairstyle. Therefore, draw in the front strands, which lie over part of the hair and the forehead, at the end. Basically, follow this simple rule: always draw the underlying shapes first, and the shapes that lie above them afterwards. That way you won't get confused.

Fine, thin strands and hair give the hairstyle further brilliance!

Since the light comes from above, it adds shadows to the lower sides of the strands. Particularly exciting are those shadows that the front strands cast on the forehead.

The strands themselves have their own shadows on the lower side and at the same time cast a drop shadow on the forehead at a slightly larger distance. On the face, there are shadows on the inside of the eyes below the eyebrows, under the upper eyelid, below the tip of the nose, below the lower lip, and below the chin and ear.

Along the outer line of the face, I also add some gray. This gives the drawing additional depth.

Now I color the hair, eyebrows and eyes with a base tone. I keep the shading.

In traditional drawing, however, it is advisable to draw in the hair base color first. Only then does the shading follow. I did it the other way around in this example to better show where exactly I place the shadows. Anyway, when drawing digitally, it is easier to do the complete shading first.

For this I set the layer with the shadows to "Multiply". Below that I color the hair on its own layer with a solid color. The shadow is automatically adjusted darker by the setting "Multiply".

So far, we have usually drawn the highlight on the hair as a simple stripe. The basic shape is always such a round light stripe that runs around the hairstyle. Now we'll get a bit more detailed and break the light stripe into small areas.

These small areas of light are within individual strand shapes. This time, try not to draw the light accents too white. Often it looks much more pleasant if the light areas are just a tad lighter than the hair itself.

LEVEL 4 – SEINEN

For those who don't always want to draw sweet and cute manga characters, in the next chapter we'll look at a more pragmatic and serious drawing style, also called *seinen*.

Optimally, you practice and learn as a drawer approaches of different styles. Many "styles" differ from each other only in the proportions of the figures. Depending on the style, the characters appear younger or older, or have cuter or more serious features.

In strong contrast to the chibi characters, the following figure has little forehead and a lot of "mass" in the middle and lower face. A rather serious looking fellow.

CHAPTER 7

SEINEN MAN FROM THREE ANGLES

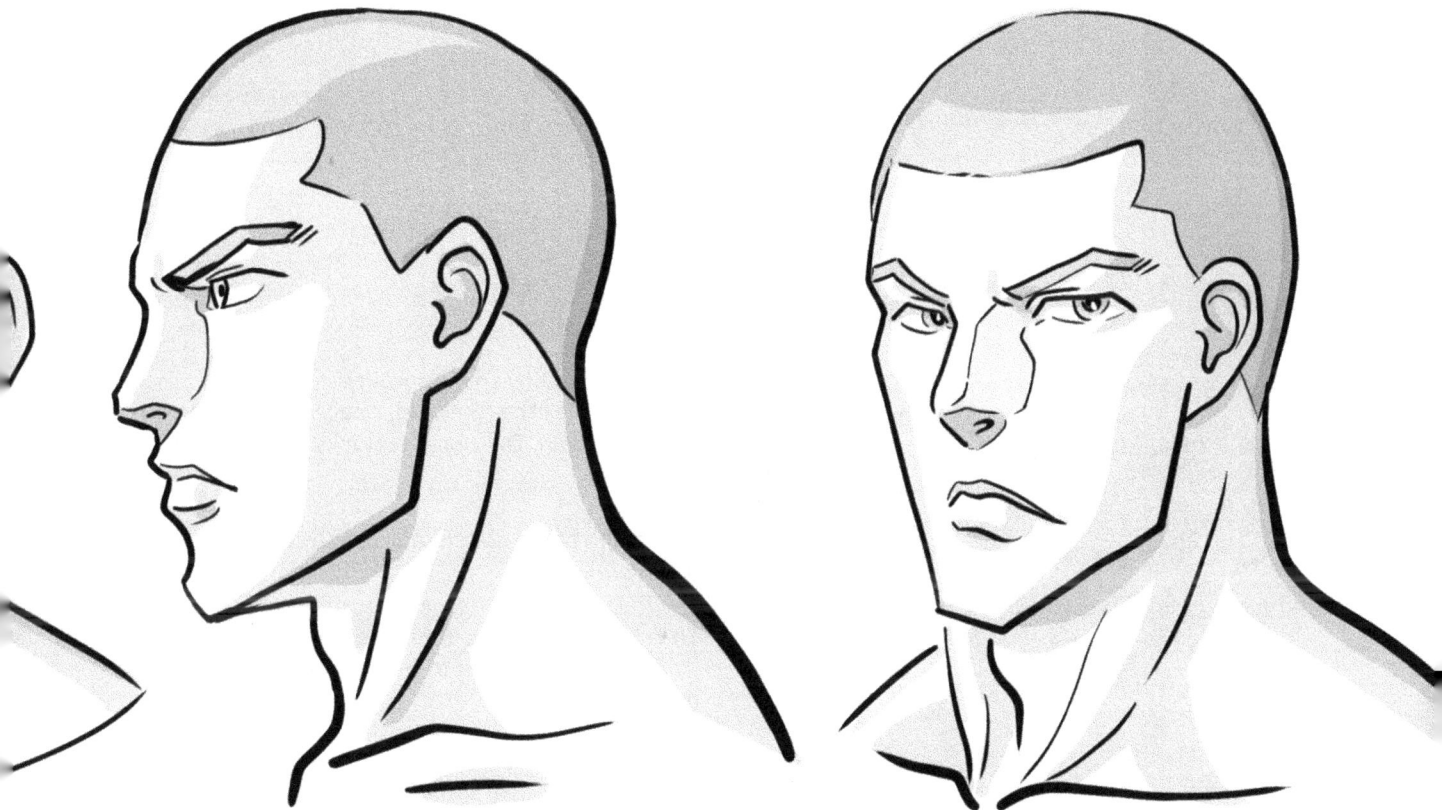

7.1 SEINEN MAN: FRONT VIEW

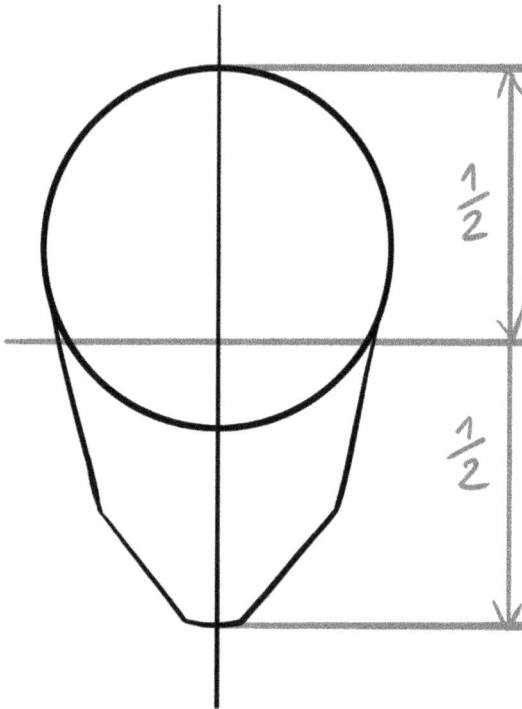

$\frac{1}{2}$

$\frac{1}{2}$

The eyes are above the horizontal central axis.

Thus we have little forehead, smaller eyes, a longer nose and a long chin.

The character looks much more adult right away.

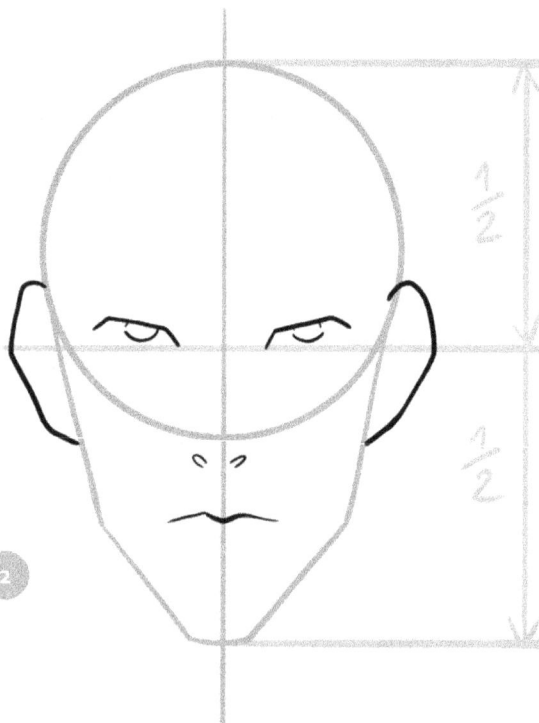

$\frac{1}{2}$

$\frac{1}{2}$

The eyes are above the horizontal central axis. Thus we have little forehead, smaller eyes, a longer nose and a long chin. The character looks much more adult right away.

The length of the nose is indicated by drawing in the nostrils.

The middle line of the mouth has the shape of a flying bird and is closer to the nose than to the tip of the chin.

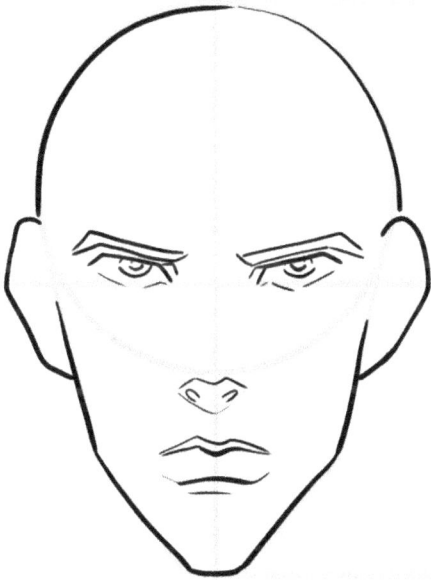

The eyebrows are close to the eyes. The iris and pupils are located in the upper part of the eye and are largely hidden by the upper eyelid. This makes the look more matter-of-fact and less playful, making the face more serious and less sweet.

The nose gets a shadow outline in the lower area. In the manga, it's quite typical to suggest the shadow there. Here you can see this shape in more detail now.

Note the comparatively large lower lip in relation to the upper lip on this character.

I'm leaving out elaborate hair for this character so we can focus more on the face. That's already complex enough. However, with this drawing you already have a super template to give him a matching hairstyle later. The outline drawing is complete after drawing in details on the ear and the side nose shadow line.

The width of the neck is somewhat exaggerated in this figure. But hey: It's still manga after all!

To practice the drawing of muscles, I recommend drawing coarser and larger at first anyway. That way, you get a feel for the shapes and can gradually draw the anatomy finer and finer.

Note that the shoulder muscles continue behind the neck. Therefore, the lateral neck lines run into the shape of the shoulder muscles.

The sternocleidomastoid muscles can be indicated clearly, but with a thin line.

5

For the shading in this case we assume that the light comes from the front. This way, we can easily draw in the three-dimensional structure. The right and left outside of the character is covered by shadow all around.

The interesting edge of the shadow is the inner one. On the head, the shadow is round and runs to the eyebrow. To the right and left, slightly below the eye, the cheekbone bulges out.

From the cheekbone, the shadow merges into the jaw and chin area.

6

Now, we have drawn in all the lateral shadows. Next, we will draw downward shadows that appear due to protruding shapes. These are below the eyebrows, upper eyelids, nose, upper lip, and below the lower lip.

Very important, of course, is the large drop shadow from the chin/jaw to the neck. The shadow on the larynx is optional, depending on how much you want to emphasize it.

Everything that is left white on the character now is called the light area. Everything we have colored gray is the so-called shadow area.

7

Finally, we color the hair and eyebrows so that they stand out against the skin. Although the hair is colored in, we can clearly see where the shadow and light areas of the hair are. In the last step, I add a darker step in the shadow area. This gives the drawing more three-dimensionality.

You achieve this by making adjustments in the inner ear area, below the ears, on the inside of the eyes, just below the chin, and on the very outside of the shoulder lines.

This elaboration of the shadow and light area can theoretically be continued indefinitely. The more gradations you add, the more realistic your drawn face will look.

8

7.2 SEINEN MAN: SIDE VIEW

The circle construction model we used for chibi and shojo works less and less as our characters become more realistic. We can still use the circle for orientation, but many areas now also deviate from our standard model.

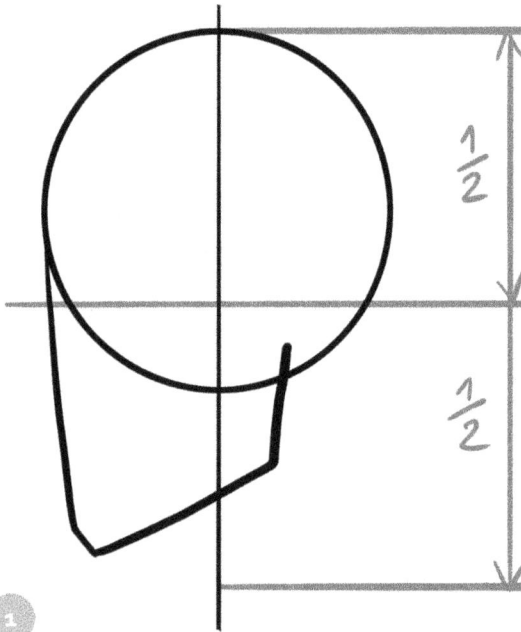

$\frac{1}{2}$

$\frac{1}{2}$

In the case of the chibi figure, the jaw line ran to the midpoint where the two center lines meet.

In this case, we have quite a pronounced face in the lower area. The jaw is massive. Therefore, the jaw line goes past the vertical midline and runs closer to the right edge of the circle.

Pay particular attention to the tip of the chin. This should not simply be pointed, but in this case should have a certain width.

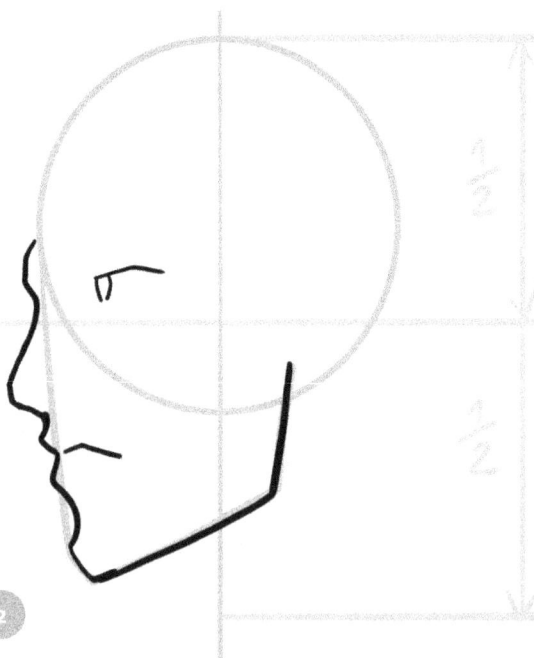

The eye bulge is very pronounced in this figure, creating a distinct bulge to the left of the eye in profile. This bulge always has something animalistic about it. The character appears physically stronger and more ready to fight, which is why this characteristic is often associated with a strong musculature.

From this eye bulge, there is a staircase down to the nose, lips and chin. This part of the face is rather flattened in simplified manga styles. Here, however, it is drawn very multifaceted, with many indentations and protuberances.

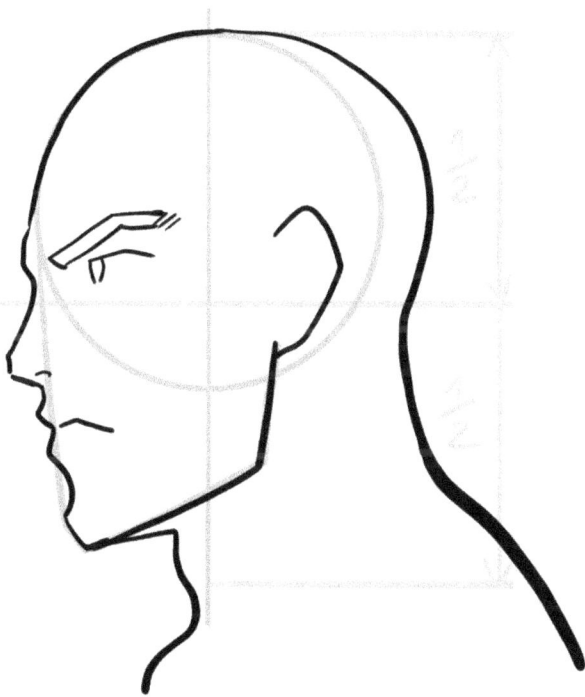

Since this character symbolizes a lot of physical strength, he also needs a wide neck. For this reason, the circle is no longer enough to define the shape of the back of his head.

We draw the back of the head wider than the circle is and show the wide neck and strong shoulder muscles.

The eye is unusually wide in the face. This again reinforces the seriousness of his gaze. The eyebrow hangs low over the eye, quite the opposite of the otherwise open and large eyes of a shojo/shonen character.

Now we define the subtleties of the face with thin lines. The lateral nose line gives the nose more structure. The shadow line below the nose gives more depth. The upper lip and lower lip give the mouth more character. The hairline has an angular shape. I especially like the corner that points to or runs parallel to the eyebrow.

A tip for advanced photographers: If you look at an eye from the side, you can usually still see the inner part of the eye, the so-called tear trough. This can be seen to the left of the iris. It is a small detail, but it gives the eye a certain realism.

In the next step, we draw in the sternocleidomastoid muscles and the collarbone. However, we only hint at both. From this perspective, it is not necessary to draw these two elements completely.

At the same time, it now becomes clearer why the laryngeal line was suddenly so bulged out at the bottom: that's where the collarbones start and the rib cage begins.

Since the character is physically very active, he has large lungs and correspondingly a large chest. This characteristic could also be reinforced by large nostrils, with which the character takes in a lot of air. Here I have omitted this, because it would simply not look as cool.

The next step is the shading. First, we draw in the shadow on the side. The light comes from the front and illuminates all shapes that can be seen from the front. Everything that curves away from the light thus falls into the shadow.

To always know exactly which areas belong in the shadow, you need a good knowledge of anatomy and a lot of experience. Therefore, just draw along first. This will give you a better feeling for shading. Gradually, you can expand this feeling with more knowledge.

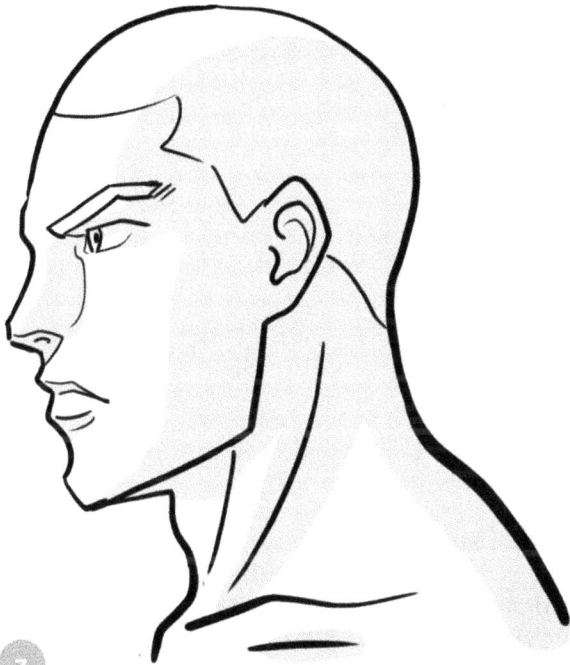

7

In the second shading step, I add all the shadows that fall down. This makes it clearer that the light is not coming directly from the front, but somewhat from above. This is a more natural light situation. Because, of course, the sun is always hanging overhead. The same is true - at least in most cases - for light bulbs and other lamps.

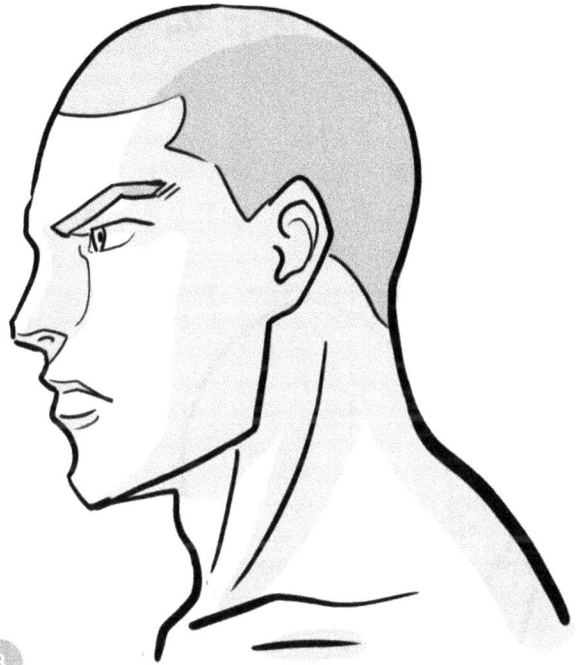

8

In the third step, I add some dark color to the eyebrows. In doing so, I keep the previously defined shading.

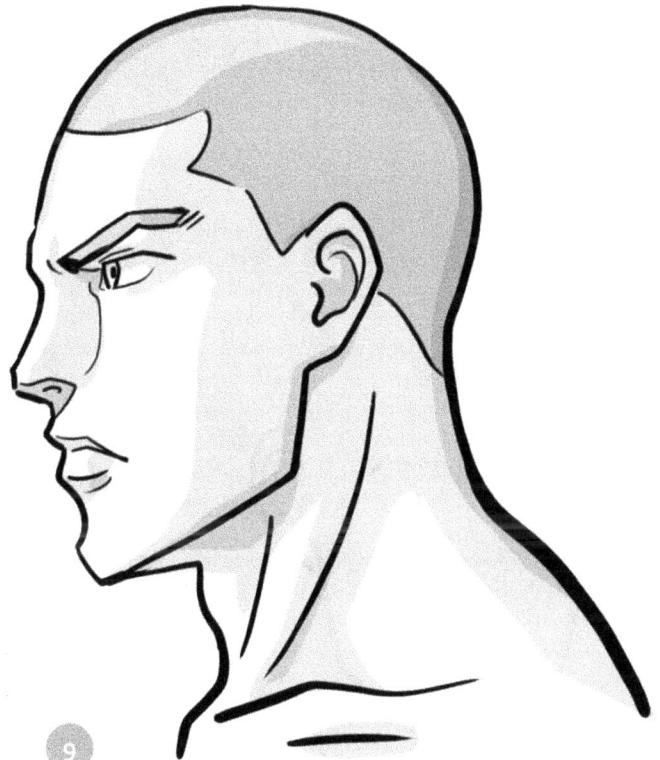

9

In the last step, I add another shadow. Inside the ear, to the left of the eye, below the nose, below the chin and along the back line of the head and neck.

7.3 SEINEN MAN: ¾ VIEW

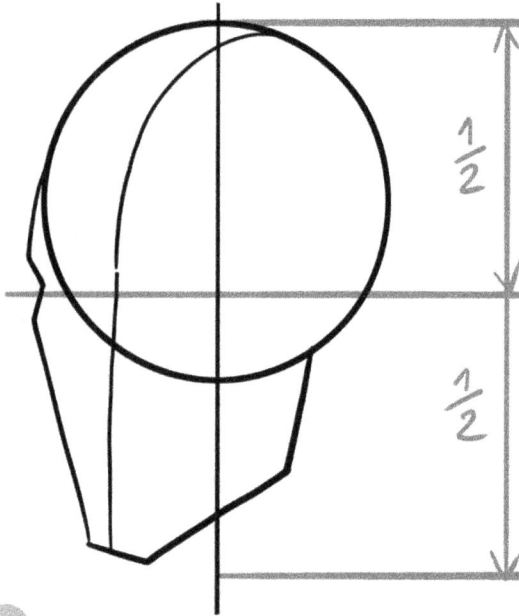

Start again with a circle.

Then draw a line from the forehead to the chin and jaw. Note that the eyes are slightly above the center line. At the level of the eyes is the crease between the eyebrow bulge and the cheekbone.

Add an approximate centerline from the middle of the chin up over the entire head. This will guide you better when drawing the perspective.

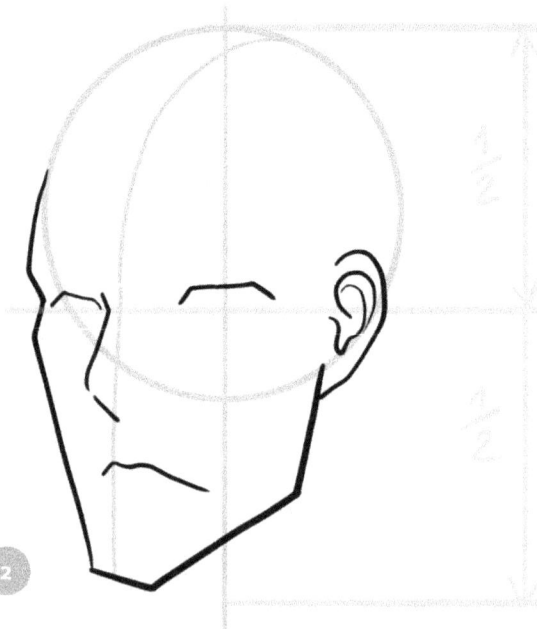

The eye bulge is very pronounced in this figure, creating a distinct bulge to the left of the eye in profile. This bulge always has something animalistic about it. The character appears physically stronger and more combative, which is why this characteristic is often associated with strong musculature.

From this eye bulge, there is a staircase down to the nose, lips and chin. This part of the face is rather flattened in simplified manga styles. Here, however, it is drawn very multifaceted, with many indentations and bulges.

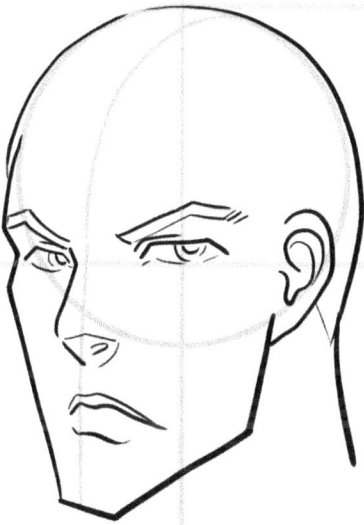

3

Be careful not to draw the eyes too big. The pupils are also rather simplified and inconspicuous. The main focus in the foreground is rather the massive chin and the broad neck.

4

This drawing is already quite advanced. Try to create a balance between thin and thick lines. Use my drawing as a guide.

IMPORTANT TIP:

If you have a hard time recognizing the shapes, look again at the chapter "Drawing the neck" (3.1).

5

Now, gradually work out the details in the face. One difficult point that I want to go into extra is the neck. From this perspective, the back of the sternocleidomastoid muscle curves around the neck – almost like a scarf. Be sure to draw in the jugular notch (where the collarbones meet) quite far to.

⑥

⑦

⑧

Continue with the lateral shading to define the basic shape of the figure. Pay particular attention to the shading on the right eye. There is a shadow below the eye. This gives the eye more roundness. The ear is completely in shadow.

The sternocleidomastoid muscles are so large that they get their own lateral shadows. Now follows the shading of the lower forms. The lower side of the nose, the complete upper lip, the lower side of the lower lip and the area below the chin get a shadow.

Now we darken the hair, eyebrows and eyes.

9

In the last step, more dark shadow areas are added.
These are on the inside of the eyes, below the jaw, on the inside of the ear,
below the ear and finally along the right side of the head and shoulder.

Drawing in perspective is a great milestone in artistic development. At least that's how I felt. At the beginning, I had a lot of trouble recognizing when something was foreshortened and when something was enlarged. And more importantly, by how much!?

When it comes to perspective, it really is often a matter of feeling, because not everything can be calculated or constructed so easily. This makes practice and repetition especially important in this area. And as far as skewed drawings are concerned: Don't get demotivated! It will get better. :)

CHAPTER 8

PERSPECTIVE DRAWING

8.1 PERSPECTIVE FROM ABOVE

In perspective drawing, we can no longer use only horizontal and vertical lines for construction. The perspective lines curve and are rounded. Let's approach the topic with some exercises.

THIS CUP WILL HELP YOU IMMENSELY UNDERSTAND THE FOLLOWING DRAWINGS.

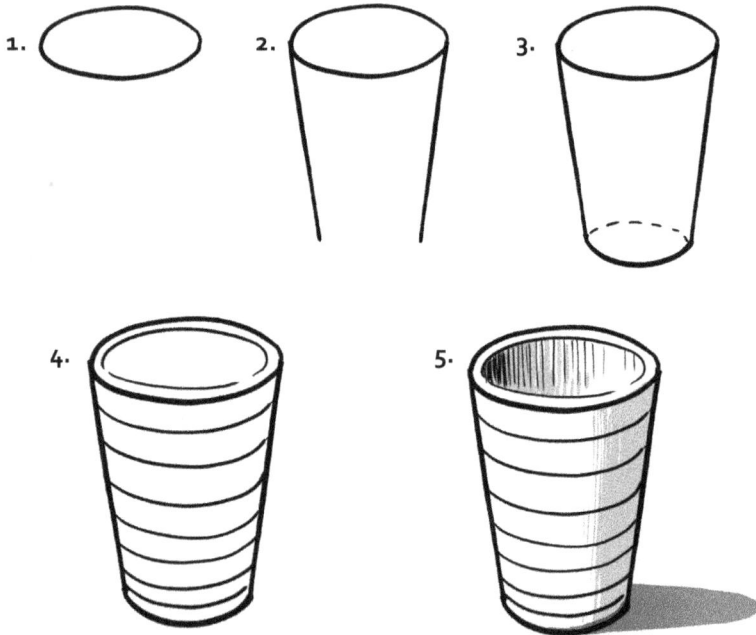

1. We see the cup from above and draw the upper ellipse-shaped opening first.

2+3. Now draw the sides that end in a smaller ellipse. From this angle, only the front area of the bottom of the cup can be seen.

4. Draw rings on the cup. These kind of lines will also serve as perspective lines for faces. Therefore, practice them well and try to draw them as parallel and clean as possible.

5. Shading.

FOR THE NEXT EXERCISE, WE WILL RESORT TO THE HELP OF THE ROBO-KUN.

The Robo-kun's head is square, which helps us approach a perspective head in a simplified way.

1. Viewed from above, we see the upper surface, that is, the upper area of the head. Hatch this area, this will make Robo-kun much more three-dimensional.

2+3. Towards the bottom, Robo-kun's head becomes narrower. The neck is only partially visible. The end of the neck resembles the cup-bottom line.

4. The eye line, which would be in the middle of the head without perspective, has sunk down quite a bit.

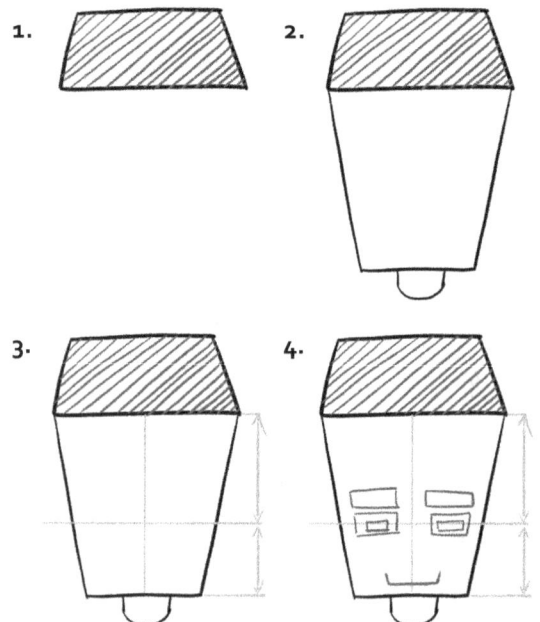

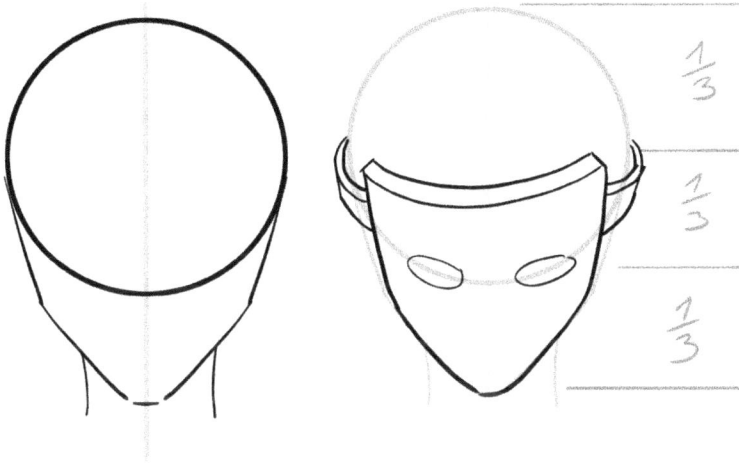

In the Robokun, the upper surface and the front surface with the face are easy to distinguish. With the head, the principle is the same. The only difference is that we no longer have such clear edges and surfaces. Everything becomes rounder and more uneven.

A good way to start is to draw in a mask for the face. This way we can better grasp the perspective and don't forget to draw in enough of the upper head area.

Most mistakes in this perspective happen because you draw in too little back and top of the head.

Too little head and too much chin will damage this perspective. The area between nose and chin is very small here.

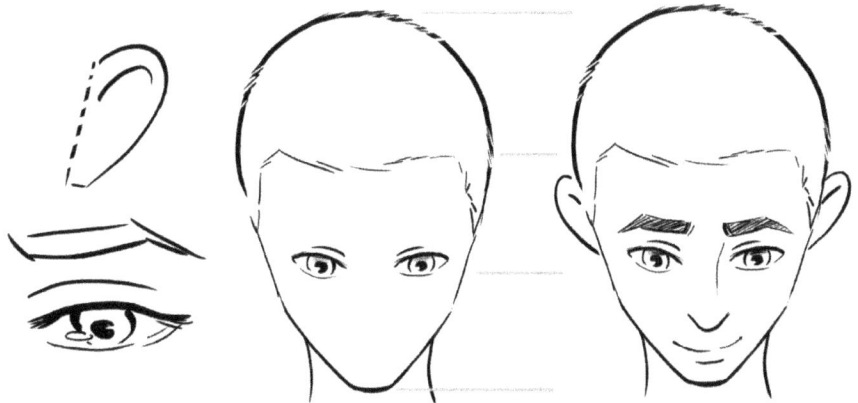

The eye line is located in the lower third of the entire head shape. Normally, we would have placed the eye line about in the middle of the face. Now the face is strongly "slipped" and compressed.

With the shading, I emphasize the upper part of the shoulders and the upper part of the head. By doing this, I set boundaries in those places where there are edges and the shape rounds out in a different direction.

The nose looks relatively long from this perspective, while the eyes and mouth area are strongly compressed.

On a more realistic drawing, you can see the changes in the shapes a little better. Therefore, be sure to draw them as an exercise.

Similar to the cup exercise, all elements of the face lie on rounded perspective lines.

Everything curves around the face. The distance between the nose and mouth is particularly tight for large noses.

Drawing a chibi character from above is a great exercise for this topic. Here, it is a little easier to estimate the distances correctly.

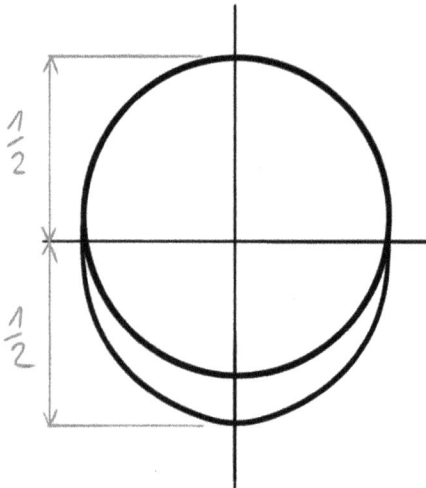

First draw a circle and then add a very small rounded jaw-chin area.

The eyes and mouth are very close to the jaw-chin line - well below the bisecting horizontal-right facial line.

The hair adds length to the back of the head and supports the perspective. The ears "move" upward in this perspective and lie clearly above the eyes.

Now, we come to an even more challenging drawing:
A 3/4 view seen from above. This gives us perspective downwards and to the right. So the details deform in two directions at once.

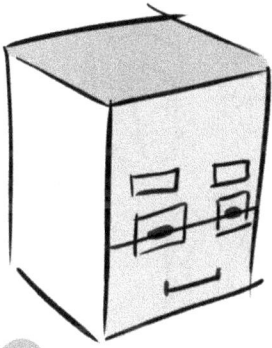

A Robokun cube head is a welcome help to make it easier for the brain to understand this view in three dimensions. Note the relevance of the different colors for the different faces of the cube. The light comes from the left and illuminates the left side. The right side and the top side are not directly illuminated, but must have different darknesses to give the impression of a clear three-dimensionality.

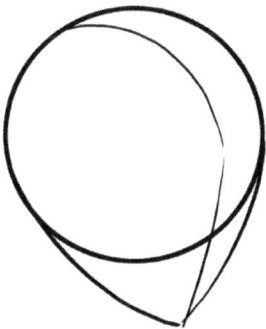

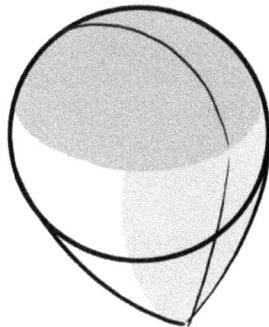

The head of our manga character is not as angular, but has basically the same structure. It has a side, a front and a top surface. This reminds us of a motorcycle helmet or the head of a doll. That's exactly right!

I started with a circle. Then I add the chin and the middle line that runs across the entire head.

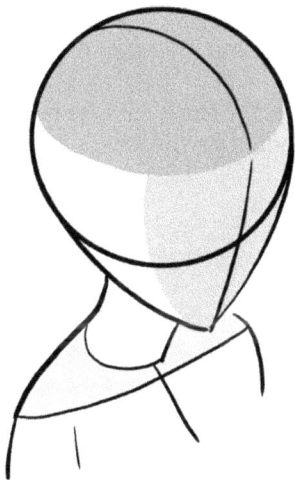

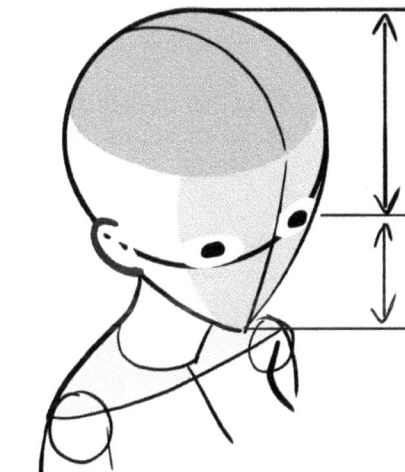

It's a coincidence, but the bottom line of the circle fits great as the perspective line of the eyes. Note that the eyes are on a slant, not a horizontal line. The line of the shoulders is also oblique and parallel to the eye line.

Seen from above, the eyes are relatively far down. We see much of the top of the head from this perspective.

6

7

Draw the oblique perspective lines and keep them as long as possible. You can align the eyebrows, eyes, nose, mouth, hairline, shoulders and chest on these lines. As soon as you draw only one shape not according to these lines, the face will look crooked and inconsistent.

Don't hurry too much with the hair. Only after you are satisfied with the face, should you move on to drawing the hair.

8

Note that the line of the bob, i.e. the front hair area by the forehead, also lies on an slanted perspective line.

The shading is quite "normal" at first. The hair around the ear, the hair on the forehead and the area under the chin are shaded.

What is new is that I have now drawn in a lot of shadow on the back shoulder of the figure. This way, we achieve a stronger three-dimensionality.

And very importantly, we create distance and depth between the chin and the back shoulder.

The distance between the chin and the back shoulder is large when we think three-dimensionally. To represent this distance on a two-dimensional drawing, we need contrasts. The shoulder is in shadow and dark, while the chin is very light. This contrast suggests a certain depth.

The hair highlight runs pretty much along the edge between the left side of the head, the front side of the head and the top side of the head. Look at the initial construction of the Robokun or motorcycle helmet head for this. This edge is round, of course, because the head is quite round. But the position is the same and can be explained. The hair highlight is not randomly placed, just as the shadows are not random. I won't go into all the details here, because that would require advanced knowledge of anatomy.

It is important that you first get used to perspectives and gain experience. Parallel to the exercises, try to acquire more and more knowledge on the subject. This way, you will improve very quickly.

128

8.2 PERSPECTIVE FROM BELOW

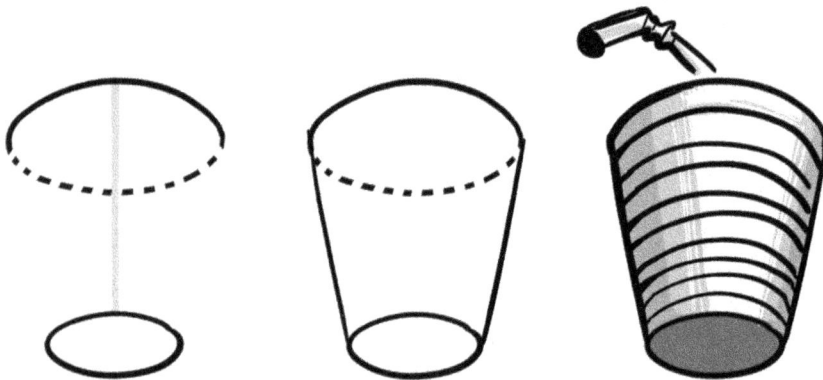

In the perspective from below, the bottom of the cup is particularly important. The upper opening of the cup, on the other hand, we no longer see at all. The perspective lines around the cup bend in the opposite direction to the perspective from above. Be sure to draw this exercise - preferably several times. The more ellipses and perspective lines you draw, the better the results!

ROBO-KUN IN PERSPECTIVE FROM BELOW

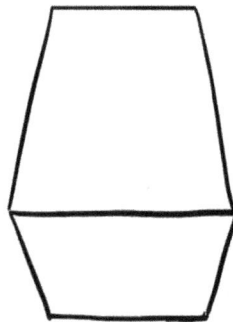

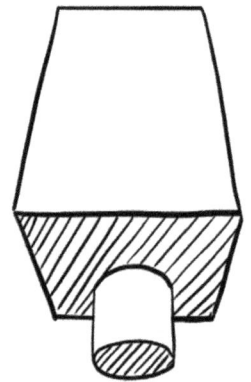

Robo-kun also shows the lower surface of his square head. The neck has the shape of a cylinder and shows, similar to the cup, an elliptical area at the bottom.

Shade these two lower areas to indicate that they are parallel to each other and at the same angle to the light.

The eyes, eyebrows and mouth shift upward. The forehead is barely visible. The lower part of the face is dominantly set in scene.

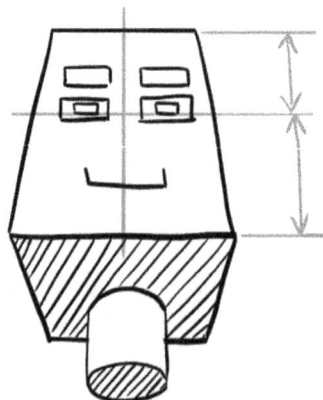

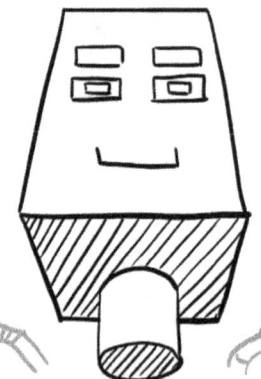

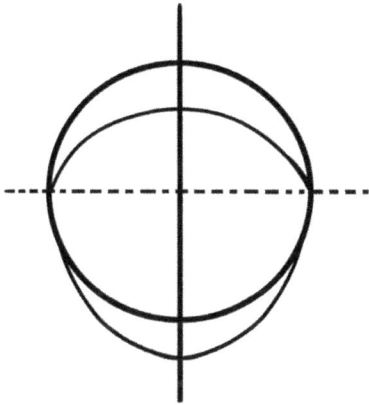

I start the construction with a circle and the two center lines. The horizontal circle centerline is dashed here.

Next, I add an area at the bottom. This is the transition between the chin and the neck.

The eye line is rounded upwards and starts at the intersections between the dashed center line and the circle.

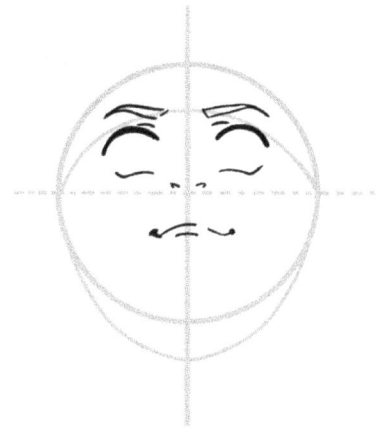

There is hardly any forehead to be seen and also relatively little hair above the forehead is visible. After all, most of the hair is on the top of the head and you can't see it from this perspective.

The iris and pupils are drawn relatively high up in the eye. There is a lot of space left between the iris and the lower eyelid. This reinforces the impression that the eye is seen from below.

The clothes and the shoulders follow the perspective lines curved upwards. The shading helps perspective when emphasizing the lower sides of the shapes.

For the Robokun, we shaded the underside of the neck and head. In this case, we're shading the underside of the hair, nose, and chin.

That's why it's so important to be able to visualize everything in three dimensions. To know where an underside is and where a shape sticks out. This is not only essential for shading, but also for line drawing.

The upper eyelids are very accentuated when viewed from below. You can clearly see their width. The pupil is quite close to the upper eyelid. The lower eyelid is drawn straight or somewhat curved upwards. The line is thin and interrupted.

The nose has a triangular shape from below, with the tip of the nose at the level of the eyes. So don't draw it too far down!

In the mouth, the upper lip in particular is very clearly visible. The lower lip is rather flattened and indistinct.

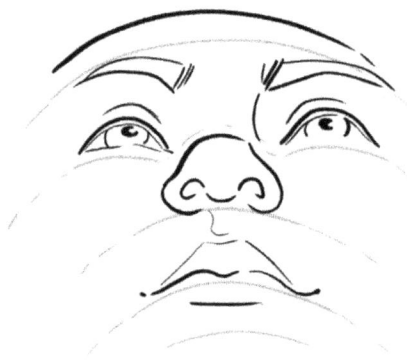

The eyebrows have more distance from the eyes and almost meet the brow line.

Let's imagine an oblique perspective from below. After all, a manga would be very boring if faces were only seen directly from below. Unfortunately, the most natural angles are also the most difficult to draw.

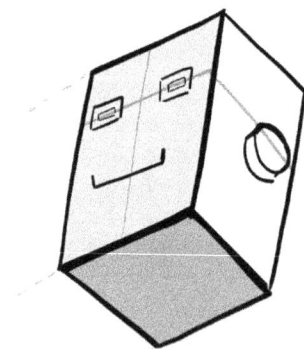

Robo-kun comes to the rescue to show a simplified version of the view.

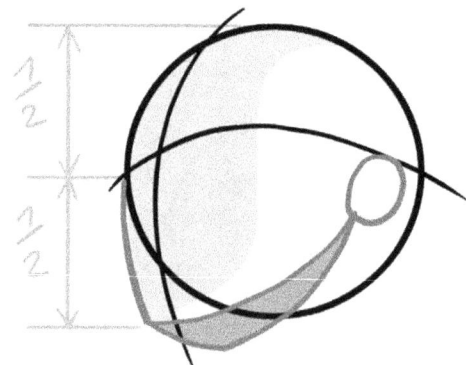

The eye line and the center line are curved at the helmet head.

First I drew a circle. Then the chin area was inserted with a bottom (shaded). This was followed by the two curved lines for eyes and for the center of the face. The eye line curves around the round head towards the ear.

From the ear we draw the neck line. The shoulder line starts slightly above the end of the neck line. This is because the shoulder muscle continues behind the neck.

The shoulders and the lower ends of the neck are on oblique perspective lines. These are roughly parallel to the front side of the eye line. Throughout the drawing, you should use very similar perspective lines so that everything on the figure is in the same perspective as much as possible.

The jawline is only hinted at. Of course, you can emphasize the chin as it suits the character, but in this case I decided that it was enough. The back cheek and chin line starts behind the nose and merges with the left neck line. The clothes rest on the shoulders and follow their shape.

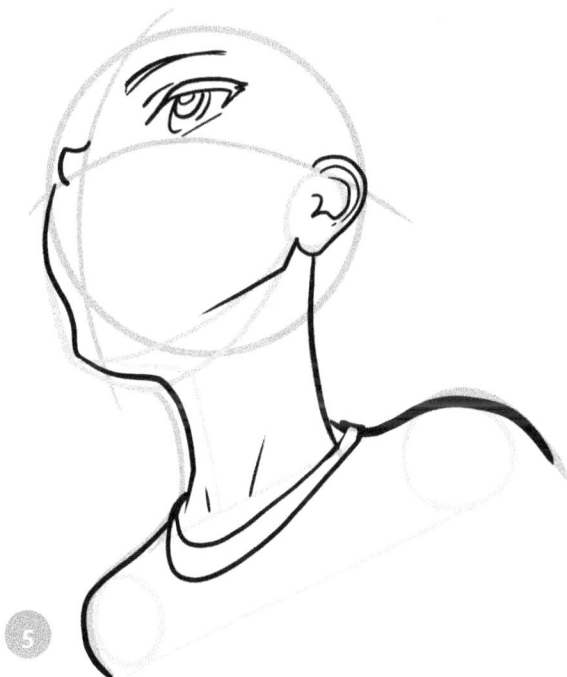

The right eye touches the eye line with its underside. It is squeezed and the pupil is relatively far up. The eyebrow is very close to the brow line, which is part of our circle. The nose is also just above the eye line - very far up. We can just leave out the back eye in this case. This looks better and we have less work.

6

Again, be careful with the strands above the forehead. Do not draw the hair too far up, otherwise the perspective will be lost.

7

The open mouth seen from below shows the upper teeth.

The collar rounds around the cylindrical neck and has the same line shapes as the cup from the same perspective.

8

The shading here follows our standard. Whereby I have placed the back shoulder more in the shade.

The open mouth is an interesting place. First, shade the entire mouth except for the front row of teeth with a medium shade of darkness.

Then shade the oral cavity behind the tongue and around the teeth darker. A light shadow on the back of the tongue indicates that some light is entering the mouth. You could even place a point of light on the tongue, but be careful not to make it too bright.

The highlight in the hair has little space in this perspective, since only a little of the hair can be seen. That's why we draw the light line rather thin and with low contrast.

So it's best not to be too white, but just take on a lighter tone of the hair color. Everything away from us has less and less contrast. Everything closer to us has strong contrasts and strong lines.

The shoulders and chin are closer to us and therefore are drawn darker and with more contrast. When you look outside into the distance, you see everything in the distance indistinctly, as if behind a blue haze. Keep this principle in mind when drawing manga characters.

Now is a good time to turn to the topic of facial expressions. So far we have dealt with the neutral face and learned about drawing in perspective. These are the best prerequisites to now continue with the facial expressions and emotions of figures!

An emotion does not only take place in the face, but is usually expressed through the whole body. The head moves in perspective, the body twists.

Let's go! :)

CHAPTER 9

FACIAL EXPRESSIONS

9.1 JOY

Let's now start into the world of facial expressions! First, I will explain what happens to the face when a character feels joy. Then I will go more and more into poses in combination with the face. The body is also important for all emotions. We first look at this in simplified form. Not the correct anatomy is in the foreground, but the tangible emotion! :D

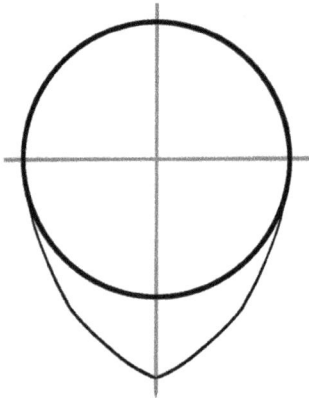

First, I'll go over the character I'm using to explain the emotions. If you like, you can trace it and use this as another exercise.

Otherwise, just draw ellipses or circles for the face and work only the face with the face with the corresponding emotion.

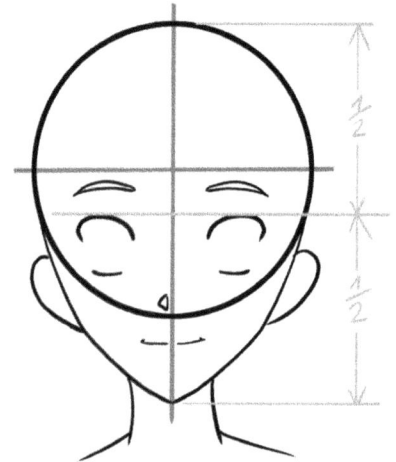

Although the girl is relaxed neutral, she looks positive. Emotions that are felt most of the time "burn" into the face, becoming the neutral expression. The corners of the mouth go up ever so slightly.

The eyebrows are relaxed.
The eyeslook joyful.

The shoulders hang down in a relaxed manner. The hair looks wellgroomed and healthy.

What happens when you smile or laugh? Try it out for yourself in front of the mirror. Which muscles move when you smile? Well, the mouth becomes wider, opens more and seems more relaxed at the same time. The teeth are not visible and the eyebrows are relaxed.

Either the eyes close completely or only partially. Especially the lower eyelid moves upwards and covers the lower part of the eye. Sometimes you can also see the upper row of teeth. However, teeth are mostly shown in attack and defense, so you should pay attention here.

The eyes have lots of sparkle. They shine with happiness. When smiling with the mouth more closed and the teeth visible at the same time, it looks as if the character has done or thought something sneaky. It is an expression of joy, but with slight ulterior motives.

A happy face has a positive and motivating effect. This is transferred to the whole body and can be supported, for example, by a thumbs up. Face and body should go hand in hand, otherwise it looks strange and it creates the impression that the person's emotion is not sincere.

When laughing out loud, the body and head are thrown backwards.
Our perspective drawing exercises from the previous chapter will help us here!

The smile on the left is supported by the hands. At the same time, the emotion has somewhat restrained. The character is shy and rather introverted.

The lower character likes it and is absolutely happy.
This complete bliss is visually underlined by the stars.

Note that for a standing character seen from a top-down perspective, the torso and legs are only indicated very briefly. The head and hands, on the other hand, are quite large, and the feet are rather small.

It is impossible to remember all the emotions. There are many subtle variations of each emotion. Therefore, collect facial expressions from different manga and anime series. That way you can quickly look up a reference while drawing.

9.2 SURPRISE AND FEAR

When a character is surprised, the eyebrows move up. Normally, this creates wrinkles on the forehead. But we don't draw them in this case because the wrinkles would make the character look too old.

The eyes are wide open. The upper eyelid in particular goes up and you can see the white of the eye between the iris and the upper eyelid.

The jaw drops down, opening the mouth. If it is neutral surprise, then the mouth has such an egg shape.

If someone is joyfully surprised, the upper area of the mouth changes. It is a combination of joy and surprise. The lower eyelid is pushed slightly upward by the smile.

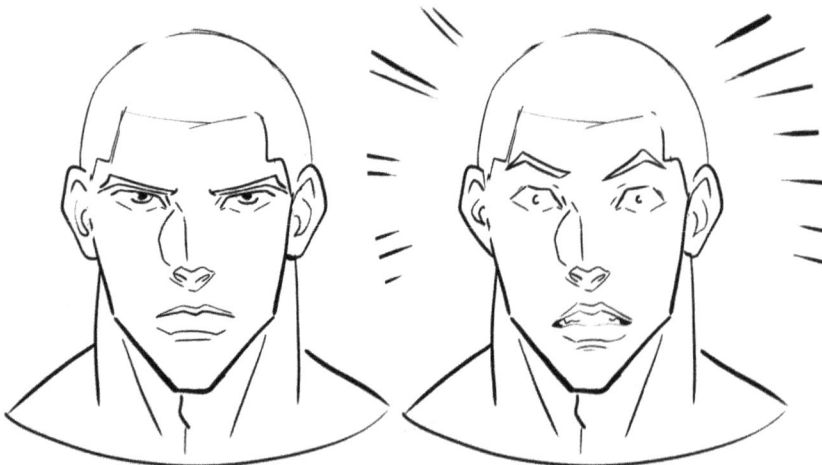

Not all characters react with the same expressiveness. This character is very surprised, but he seems composed at the same time.

His lower lip moves down, but his teeth stay together. His eyes are widened, but they are still quite small.

His body remains stiff. To make the surprise clear anyway, you can draw in motion lines, for example.

Surprise can easily turn into fear and horror. For this purpose, the eyebrows move upward, but are serious and tense.

The pupil becomes even smaller to a point. The mouth is no longer rounded, but rather angular. Especially in the lower area it is broad and angular. Vertical shadings on the forehead and under the eyes create an additional "horror effect".

This character looks very surprised, almost frightened. His whole body evades surprise. No pupils, wide open mouth and "trembling fright lines" on the head and shoulders are details that characterize this emotion.

The figure flinches with the whole body.

Here you can read disbelief, surprise and fear. The eyes are squeezed out and covered with veins. The pupils are very small.

The mouth shows teeth, which gives the surprise more of a defensive effect before an attack. However, the body does not yet move away from the source of danger.

The character can only watch in horror, but has not yet grasped the situation to the point of evading or fleeing.

This emotional expression could also pass for joy.
It is probably a mix of joy and positive surprise.

In this example, the posture of the arms is interesting.
It is a tense anticipation before a surprise.

Emotions are often combinations of different feelings.
And yes, I like drawing little stars!

This character is surprised and at the same time
somewhat disgusted and afraid. The lower mouth line
is wavy and suggests a jittering of the lower jaw.

She might have simply been startled by the buzzing of
the bumblebee and therefore feel spontaneous fear.
However, when she recognizes the bumblebee, she may
relax.

It is a brief snapshot. She is startled and dodges. At the
same time, she raises her shoulders and holds her arm
protectively in front of her.

Different characters react differently to surprise -
fearful or confident and unaffected. Every emotion has
different gradations and forms.

9.3 ANGER AND RAGE

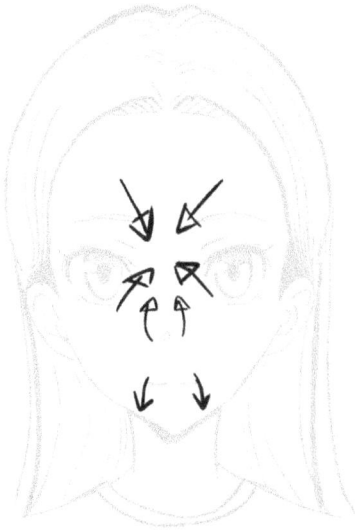

The eyebrows are pressed together and over the eyes. This results in creases between the eyebrows. The eyebrows also cover parts of the upper eye.

The eyes are compressed from below. The lower eyelid moves upward. Normally, the nostrils are also pulled up, but this is often omitted in the manga. The mouth is more compressed, the corners of the mouth move down. The chin with the lower row of teeth is pushed forward.

In case of greater, uncontrolled anger, the eyes are opened wide and teeth are shown. Bulges appear under the lower lip. Try it out on yourself: When you feel anger, you move the chin forward and "curl" it. The lower lip is tense. Due to the tension you forget to breathe and veins appear in your face.

At the next stage of anger, you tear open your mouth and scream. The eyebrows have the typical "anger shape". The pupils are empty with sheer rage.

In this chibi style it still looks cute because the teeth are not emphasized so much and many "anger wrinkles" around the mouth, eyes and nose are omitted.

In a slightly more realistic manga style, the wrinkles are visible on the inside of the eyes are visible. These go roughly in the direction of the tip of the nose.

The wrinkles on the forehead and between the eyebrows have finer lines towards the top. The eyebrows are clearly pushed down and cover the eyes. The corners of the mouth are pressed down convulsively, forming pent-up wrinkles.

Anger is also usually represented by an emphasized lower lip.
In this character it is not necessary, because he has a large lower lip anyway and thus already looks like anger.

This character is ready to fight and let the pent-up anger explode. Anger often has a lot to do with energy. This is additionally expressed here by the flying hair and the lines of movement.

This character resembles a cactus that can bite.
Its teeth are sharp and angular, its hair is spiky, its eyes are bare, and its neck is elongated. Everything about him says, "Don't touch me right now!"

Notice that the eyes are drawn extra evil here. The line of the upper eyelid slopes downward on the inside, much like the anger eyebrows.

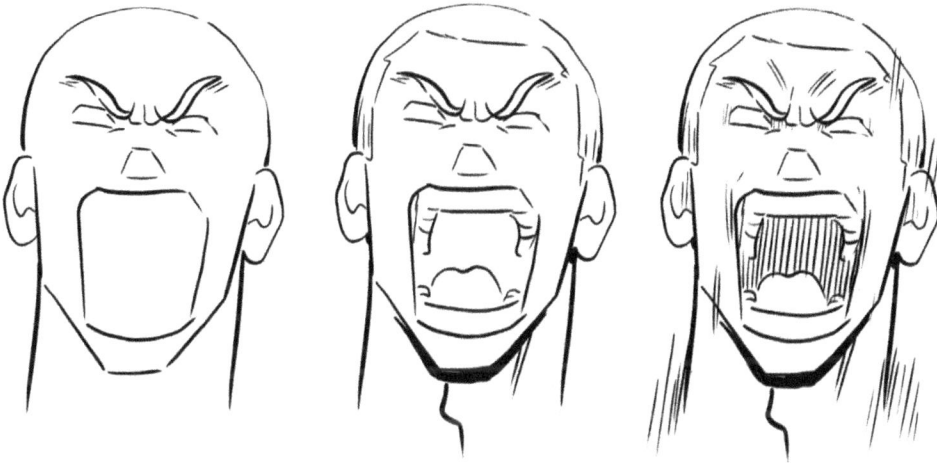

He rears up and unleashes his anger/rage energy to take it out on someone. The perspective is slightly from below. Note the small forehead, the nose from below and the visibility of the upper row of teeth.

A light annoyance of a rather introverted character, not to be taken seriously. She is trying to be angry, but it looks rather weak and sweet. A lot of insecurity resonates in this pose, and it's more of a deflection than a real letting out of anger.

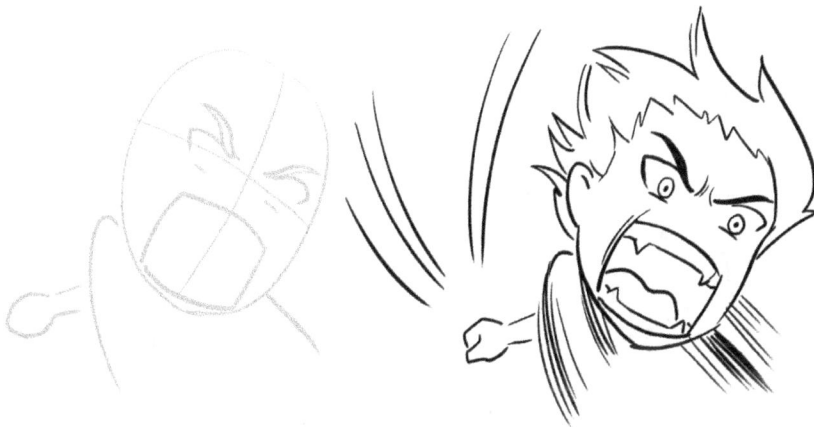

In the manga, anger plays a big role especially in fights. Many lines of movement and a torn mouth are typical elements. Also, small pupils bring a lot of drama and tension to a duel. On the other hand, imagine a fight between two happy or sad characters! That would be something different, but probably a very low-energy affair.

9.4 GRIEF

When a character is surprised, the eyebrows move up. Normally, this causes frown lines to appear.

However, we do not draw them in this case because the wrinkles would make the figure look very old.

In the case of greater sadness, the eyebrows are not only drawn upward on the inside, but also form congestion folds between them. Tears accumulate on the inner and outer sides of the eyes. They run in a curve along the round face and drip down the chin.

The trembling and shaking of the body can be suggested by broken lines around the body.

This character is not sad because of something he sees in front of him, but because he remembers something. The closed eyes indicate that he is mentally imagining something. This imagination has finally triggered the sadness.

Many highlights indicate a moist eye. The eyebrow is raised on the inner side. The lower area of the eye is obscured and indistinct by the dashed lines.

Tears accumulate on the lower eyelid, especially on the left and right edges of the eye. If too much fluid has accumulated, the tear runs down the face in the form of a drop. Draw the tear with different, rather thin strokes. After all, tears are actually transparent.

Draw a shadow under the large collections of tears to give the tears more depth. Rounded highlights on the large tears make the drawing more impressive. The tear runs down the face, leaving a thin, wet trail.

Many tears can be drawn like a waterfall. These can run along the face or shoot out of the eyes like a hose.

This character is speechless and slightly horrified. He does not shiver, but is literally frozen.

His eyes do not fix on any particular point and instead stare into the void. The jaw has dropped and the mouth is open. The tears just keep flowing, showing that this figure feels a deep sorrow.

The numbness dissolves and the sadness is now joined by anger. He wants to actively defend himself against the situation, but he is still very sad.

The eyebrows are in the "anger position".

The mouth shows a mixture of anger and sadness in this position. His eyes run red because of the anger and the many tears.

Some tears bounce off the face as he does this. This reinforces the energy behind his emotions.

She keeps her head down and is sad. We cannot tell from this attitude whether she will do something about the thing that has caused this emotion in her.

She allows the sadness to happen and doesn't fight it. Sometimes you have no choice but to let the sadness overcome you.

Here we have a very exaggerated sad facial expression – a big howl. The person does not hold back his grief, but instead lives it out openly and loudly. The mouth opens uninhibitedly, the tears flow out of the eyes in a big arc. This technique is more appropriate for an extroverted character.

Sad characters might like to cling to something that helps them find comfort.

This can be a thought, a person, or an object. Instead of the teddy bear, you can also draw something completely different.

The dynamics and the emotion behind the pose are crucial here.

What is special here is that even the outlines of the eyes are wobbly.

The lower lip is also full of waves. This wavy one goes well with the emotion of sadness. Imagine he's received some sad news and completely bursts into tears while still in the middle of reading it.

This motif is not only a good exercise to practice drawing tears, but also water in general. ;)

YOU CAN DO IT !!

With this book I want to strengthen your flexibility in drawing.
Because no matter how your art develops, it's always good to have
options and to be versatile in drawing.

The typical circle construction method for manga faces is great for
the beginning. But at some point it's important to be able to break
away from that and use freer shapes for heads.
That way you don't run the risk of always drawing too similar
characters.

CHAPTER 10

DIFFERENT HEAD SHAPES

10.1 ROUND HEAD SHAPES

We start here with the circle we are familiar with. However, the use is somewhat different in this case. This time the circle describes the entire shape of the head.

The widest part of the head is approximately at the level of the ears.

Make sure here that not only this lady's head is rounded. Her shoulders, her hands and the cake are as well. The round shapes harmonize with each other to create a coherent overall image.

NOTE: The theme of the perfect circle resonates, as it so often does in drawing. Don't let doubts stop you. Circles are just a guide and they don't have to be so extremely symmetrical. Clean lines and symmetrical shapes are hard to draw. Only advanced drafters can get it clean. So don't be discouraged if your drawing looks a little wonky at first.

Try to use as few construction lines as possible in this chapter. Instead, try to strengthen your sense of proportion and feeling when drawing. Not an easy thing to do! But with practice it will make you much more flexible in drawing.

10.2 RECTANGULAR HEAD SHAPES

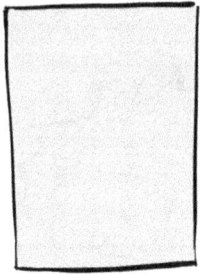

In these examples, try to use rectangles not only when drawing the head shape, but also for all other elements of the head. Eyebrows, clothes, eyes, hair and beard can also have something very rectangular.

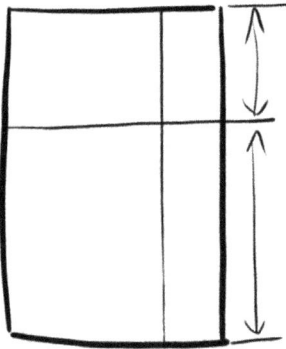

1 Notice how the hair and beard of this fellow pick up the rectangular shape of his head. This extends the shapes, but does not change them.

2 Hair is an extension of the shape of the head. That's why it's always so important to sketch the bare head f rst.

3 The hair is added after the fact.

4

5 This character looks like a blacksmith or a martial arts master. Definitely someone who likes to be physically active. The angularity and a wide, large chin are elements of the face that visually express his physical strength. In addition, of course, there is the wide, muscular neck.

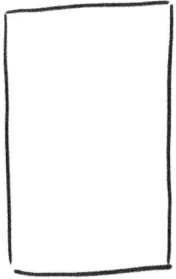

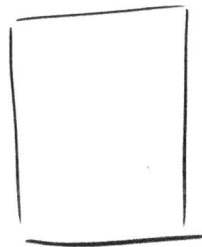

The "rectangular heads" do not have a clearly widest point in the head.
The head is approximately the same width at all points.

10.3 TRIANGULAR AND EGG-SHAPED HEAD SHAPES

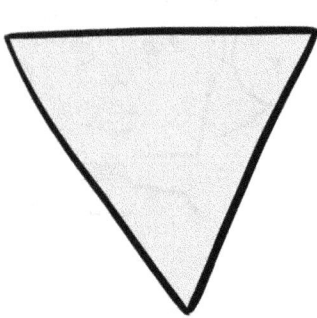

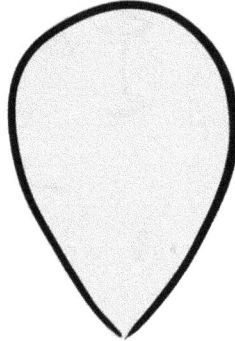

The widest point in this head shape is quite high.The forehead is high, the "brain area" is the most dominant of the head.The chin, on the other hand, is small and the jaw is narrow. How do such characters look to you?

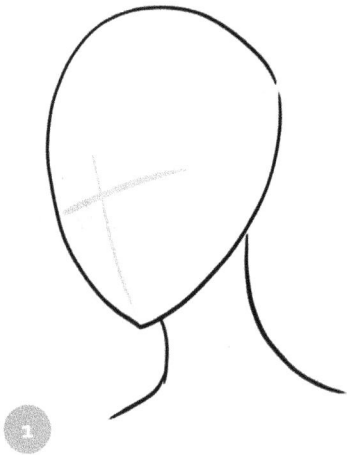

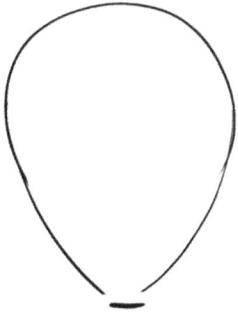

10.4 OTHER HEAD SHAPES

Here you can see a few more head shapes I came across during my research. Although the different characters that fit a head shape are so different, they still somehow have something in common. That's because the main head shape is incredibly important. If you give the characters in your story a wide variety of main head shapes, it will make the narrative seem all the more alive. Again, for practice, draw the different characters.

HEAD SHAPES: EXERCISE

Analyze the people around you. What kind of head shape do they have? Try to draw them in a simplified way. It doesn't have to look like them right away, but it strengthens your eye for your surroundings and for creating characters. Also look at anime and manga characters from series and movies and pay special attention to their head shape.

Draw at least five new characters on this page with already shown head shapes or try your hand at completely new head shapes.

When I feel uncreative, I close my eyes and simply draw scribbles. Then I let myself be inspired by the shape and try to discover a face in it. Often the craziest characters emerge that way. Try it out! :)

Unfortunately, to draw an older person, you can't just add a few wrinkles to the face. Okay, in some anime series it's actually done that way. But then it often looks very odd ...

With advancing age, many things happen to the face.
The face changes significantly. In order to understand the detailed aging process and to be able to depict it realistically, you have to deal with various exercises on this subject.

And even though there are no wrinkle lines when drawing a baby, each age has its own drawing challenges.

Let's get started! :)

CHAPTER 11

DRAWING DIFFERENT AGING STAGES

11.1 DRAWING A GRANNY

For the first exercise, we will draw simplified, older characters. These are reminiscent of chibi grannies and chibi grandpas. But even here, a lot of attention is needed. A higher age usually means more strokes. The shapes of the face become more complex, with wrinkles and bumps. But let's take a closer look!

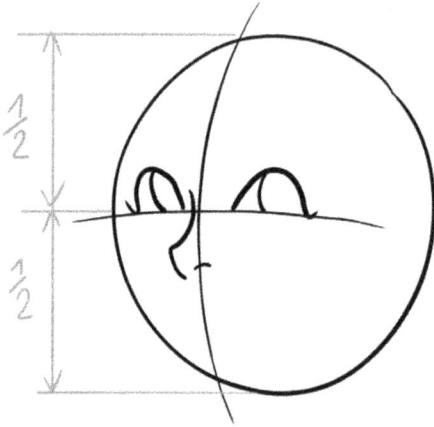

The granny will have a rather round head. Therefore, you can safely start with a circle here and see it as the head shape. Imagine you are drawing a full moon with a face. The circle is sketched loosely. It's perfectly okay if it's not perfect.

The eyes and nose do not yet reveal the age. Only when we draw in the mouth area and the wrinkles under the eyes does it become clearer.

The chin floats around independently and is inside the circle. The jawline is rarely visible in old age, but the chin is actually always visible.

The left outer line of the face is super important.
This line does not connect to the chin as it usually does,
but runs into the neck at a small distance from the chin.
The tissue weakens with age and hangs down in the jaw
area. Thus, the underlying jaw is no longer clearly
visible.

4

The right jaw line to the right of the ear downward
is only rudimentarily visible. We simply leave the
connection between the ear and the chin blank.
In this way, we indicate that the area does not show
a clear jawline. There is soft tissue over this line, which
means that there is a connection between the cheek and
the neck.

5

With age, one (usually) becomes weaker and the head is
harder to hold. The entire body is bent forward and the
neck is thus quite tilted away from the head.

Now we come to the wrinkles on the forehead, the outer
corners of the eyes (the so-called "crow's feet") and on
the neck. Be careful to indicate these wrinkles with a thin
line. Also, do not draw the wrinkles too straight, but
slightly curved. After all, the head is not square, but full
of curves.

6

Note that the grandma in this case is still very much alive and well. The shapes of the eyes, the nose and that of the ears are almost youthful. Of course, these elements could be made older. I'll show you how to do that in the later, more advanced drawings.

Practice this simplified shape first, until you are skilled at suggesting wrinkles appropriately. I put a bit of shading under the nose, under the upper eyelid, at the eyelid creases, at the ear, at the back of the neck, and at the corner of the mouth.

Also with this nice granny from the frontal view we use all mentioned key areas to make her look older. The peculiarity in this case: wrinkles above the mouth. People with a very lively or very tense upper lip develop wrinkles in this area. Draw these wrinkles with care, because they change the expression of the character very much. I think the grandma looks much sadder with the mouth wrinkles.

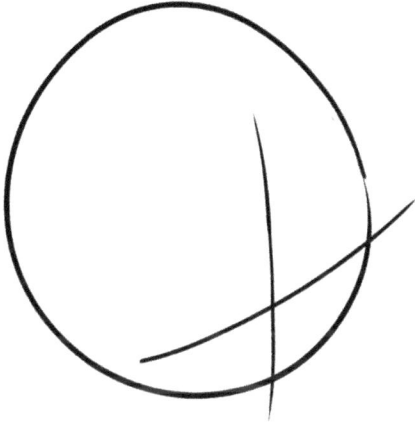

1

We see this granny slightly from above from the 3/4 view. That's why a lot of the top and back part of the head is visible.

2

The back cheek is clearly visible. We simply omit the nose and a separate chin - very much in the chibi drawing style.

3

The wrinkles on the forehead and on the side of the mouth already make her look like a granny. This shows that these are the most important wrinkles when it comes to drawing elderly people.

4

Keep in mind, though, that a grandma's hairstyle, facial expressions, and attitude also help make her a granny. (I'm sure the cake tastes delicious!! XD)

11.2 DRAWING A GRANDPA

Some people remain very cheerful in old age, such as the little granny from the previous chapter. Others become rather apathetic. Nothing can surprise them anymore. The look is then duller, no longer so lively and sharp.

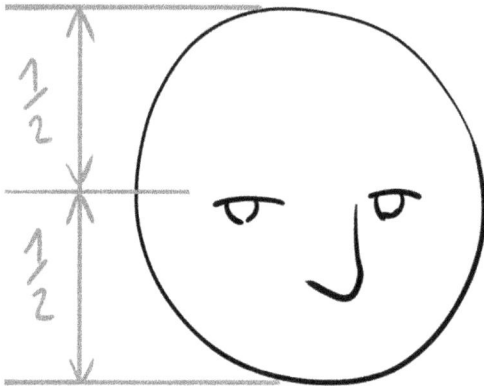

This grandpa still looks fit, but he is more emotionless than the granny. His upper eyelids hang down weakly and cover most of the eye.

The eyebrows are quite high, which shows that he at least attempts to be attentive. The lifeless expression of the eyes, on the other hand, indicates a reduced receptiveness.

The upper lip beard is convenient, so we avoid drawing the mouth. Draw a few thin strands in the beard. This makes it clearer that it is moustache hair and not an open mouth.

The ears appear larger with age. The tissue loses tension with age, which has a particular effect on the earlobes. Gravity causes them to be pulled into length.

By the way, this also applies to the nose. The nose and ears also appear larger with age because the face as a whole is more sunken. In addition, the neck becomes more shriveled. A pair of additional wrinkle lines is all that is needed here.

Some people no longer pay much attention to their hair in old age. The remaining hair above the ears of the grandfather I therefore draw here a little tangled.

This also fits well with his passive facial expression. If he would appear fashionable and styled, one could assume that someone has made him pretty. He himself, however, will be quite indifferent to this. I have only hinted at the pupils, his eyes are rather dull than lively and with a lot of highlights.

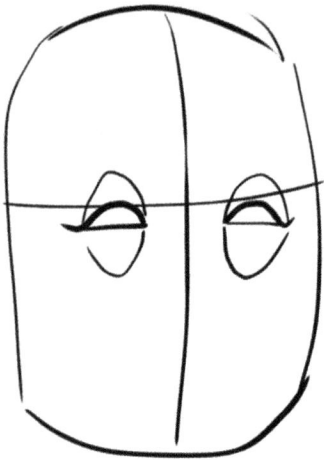

168

Next, let's draw a wise-looking Asian grandpa. This one will be a bit more detailed and won't have the typical circle as a head shape. Start with a cuboid that has rounded corners. The eyes are placed higher up. Note that the upper eyelid is quite curved and drawn with a strong line.

The eyebrows grow out of the head like little hands. The mouth no longer has visible lips and consists only of a line. The nose is rather broad at the bottom, which is why the nostrils are also drawn wide apart.

This grandpa is quite skinny. You can see how his strong cheekbones are clearly protruding. His gaze is to the left. The iris is covered by the eyelids both above and below. A common eye shape in the Asian region.

4 The ears are large and have large earlobes. In this case, the beard has a very special shape. At the base of the beard, the lines are thin and are jagged. From the base, you can draw in long strands that join at the bottom to form a point. Note here that the beard is a light beard and therefore flutters around. Its shape is not stiff, but flowing.

5 We narrow the jaw somewhat. This brings the forehead area more into focus in this drawing. A wise grandfather thinks a lot. Therefore, we should also emphasize his forehead region and weaken the jaw area a bit in return. The wrinkles between the eyebrows also show that he is often focused on his thoughts.

6 The neck of the old man is rather lean and is not too straight. The body tension eventually decreases with age. I have drawn the base of the eyebrows a little "lighter" here by interrupting the solid line. So the base is rather dashed. This way, the eyebrows no longer look pasted on. They connect more with the skin and look more natural.

7 Since I want to show that his beard and eyebrows are white, I color his skin and clothes in this case. One point of light each on his forehead and the tip of his nose bring a lot of three-dimensionality to the drawing with little effort. Shadows are especially important under the eyebrows, under the chin, and under the beard. Highlights in the eyes bring a clear look to our wise man. He still has alert thoughts and likes to share his wisdom with us.

11.3 OLDER MAN (ADVANCED LEVEL)

You may see it at first glance: This is quite an advanced and challenging drawing. Nevertheless, I decided to include it in the book because I think it's very important to dive into it in more detail – even if only briefly. The more detailed knowledge you gather, the easier it will be to draw simplified manga characters.

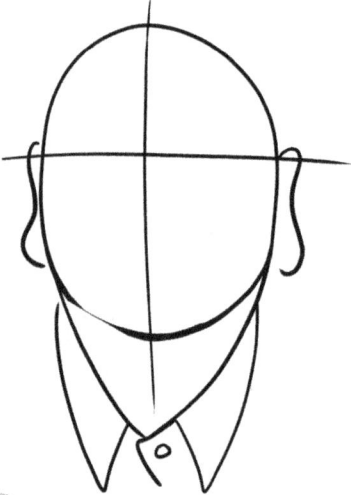

For this reason, my recommendation would be: even as a beginner, dare to do more complex drawings like this one - even without the expectation of getting everything just right. The drawing does not have to be perfect. But even a single attempt will help you to learn a lot of new things..

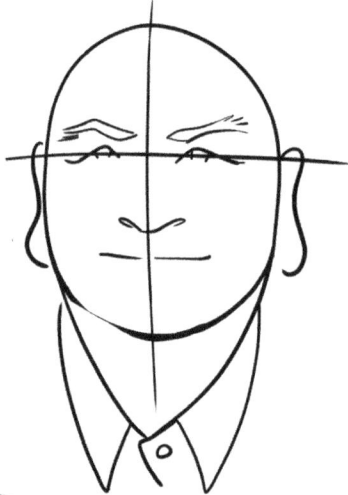

Make sure that the eyes are quite high up in the face and that they are rather small.This will make the character more adult and not cute.

The nose is quite massive, the forehead between the eyebrows is tense. The earlobes are large and protrude from the face. The jaw line between the chin and the ear is only rudimentary.

All of these are the basic shapes of the face for now. Therefore, we can use strong lines here.

Now we work out the shapes more finely. With thin lines we give the forehead more character. See how playful the crease lines are? They are not simply straight, but undulate almost uncontrollably.

The crow's feet on the eyes are just as playful. They almost form a checkered pattern.

The nasolabial fold starts quite thick at the wings of the nose and thins towards the corners of the mouth. Make sure that the nasolabial fold does not connect with the corners of the mouth, but runs past them with some distance.

Hair and ears get more detail with a thin line.

Add more fine lines on the lips and around the lips. Make sure that the lines do not run too parallel to each other. In addition, the left and right sides of the face should have different wrinkles.

Additional wrinkles are added under the mouth, on the chin and on the cheeks. The tissues of the face slump a little. As a result, indentations become visible on the cheeks. It looks like the person is pulling his or her cheeks in a bit.

Notice that most of the wrinkle lines on the face - whether on the neck, mouth, cheek or forehead - are downward.

The stare of this figure is slightly glassy and somewhat indistinct. The vision is no longer so strong and the eyes tear more easily.

In addition, pigments, warts and bumps often appear on the skin with age.What would be inappropriate on a young face can be drawn in more generously here.

That is the beauty of an older face. You can let off a little more steam artistically. I always find that quite liberating.

Here, the lines no longer have to be straight and "perfect", but can be drawn in a more playful and spidery way.

11.4 BABY FROM THE FRONT

For drawing a baby you need only a few lines. After all, babies don't have wrinkles (on their faces) and are made up of rounded shapes. Nevertheless, you need to be careful. Because of the few lines, each one has more weight.

In an elaborate drawing with a lot of hatching, you can conceal a lot with additional strokes.
In a reduced baby drawing we do not have this possibility. Therefore, pay special attention to each individual line and do not underestimate the simplified drawing.

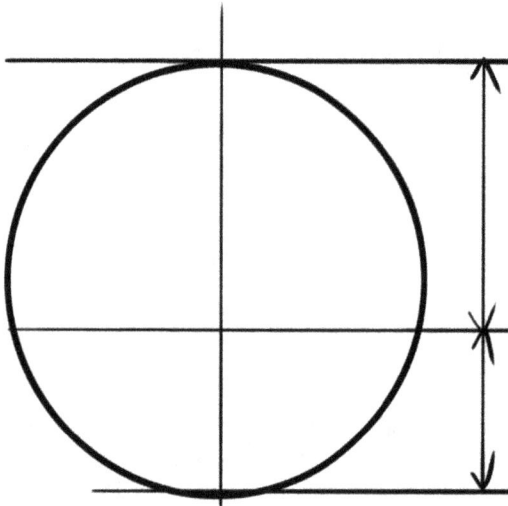

Babies in drawings resemble the classic chibi characters in their proportions.

The eyes are very far down, leaving only a very small chin area. The forehead area is very large and dominant. You know: the chibi style wants to look cute. And what is cuter than babies?

However, there are small but subtle differences between chibi characters that look like babies and actual babies.

So let's go through the front view together step by step.

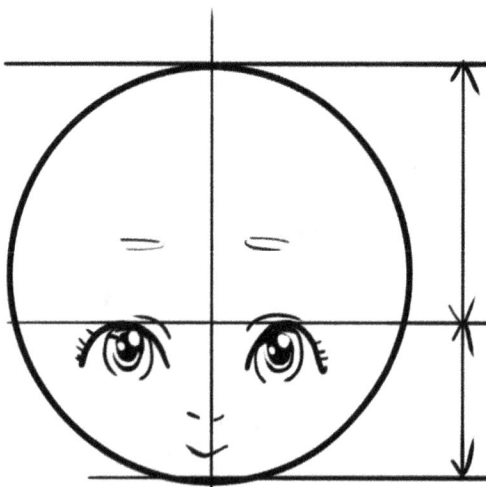

The eyes lie completely in the lower third of the head. The nose and mouth are only slightly indicated. The special feature of the mouth is that it is usually very small.

In addition, the upper lip in the baby is very playful and stands out dominantly forward. The mouth here has a V-shape. The figure does not have a definite smile on its face. The friendly look is created by the upper lip, which pushes forward strongly, almost automatically.

The eyebrows are often barely visible. That's why I've also only hinted at them and drawn them open to the outside. But of course there are variations. Some babies have very pronounced eyebrows.

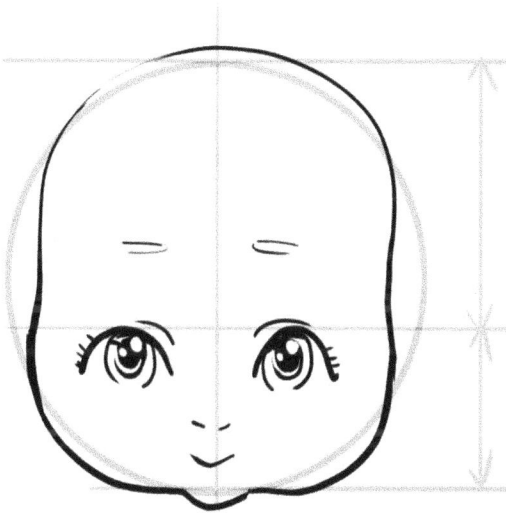

The cheeks of a baby are very pronounced. Some babies have real chubby cheeks! They bulge out at the sides. The little chin between the cheeks peeks out slightly. You could leave the chin out, but then the cheeks wouldn't stick out as much.

This is also one of the biggest differences with chibi-style characters of any age. There, the chin is usually left out and the cheeks are drawn a bit flatter.

A neck is hardly visible on a baby's head. The shoulders and the whole body are very small overall. The first hair of a child is often slightly curly.

Therefore, it actually fits well to draw babies with curly hair. Since the hair (often) forms only in places at the beginning, it is enough to give the baby a curl in the front.

This is a simple visual way to show that the hair is not fully formed and the baby is very young, for example, an infant.

11.5 BABY FROM THE SIDE

Seen from the side, the baby head has some distinctive features. Initially, it is very similar to a chibi head. The big eye is very far down.

The ear is also low and the jaw line is rounded.

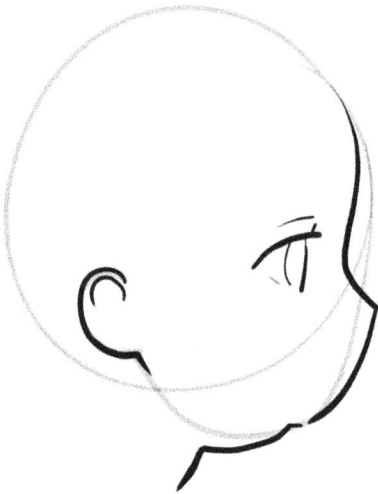

The nose is a little snub nose. The forehead is rounded and high. It even bulges out to the right. It is not a receding forehead.

Something very special is the course from the chin to the ear. Here we have usually drawn a direct connection before. In the baby, however, everything is very soft in this area. A large cheek and a double chin go directly into an almost invisible neck.

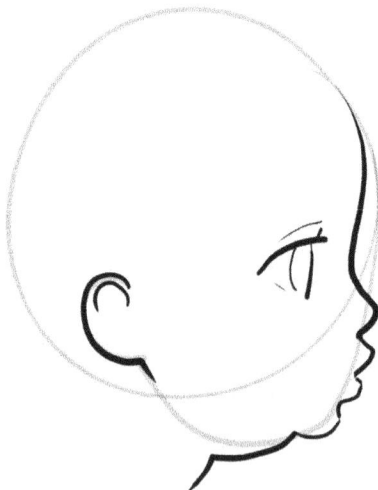

The upper lip sticks out very far. This makes the baby look even cuter. Also, make sure to draw rounded and cute shapes.

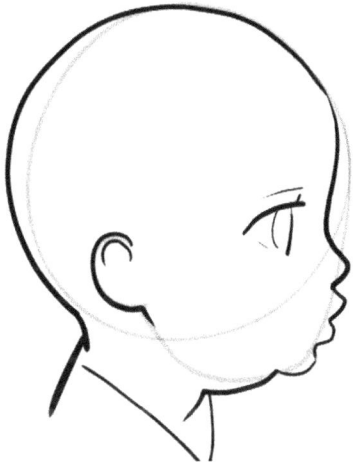

Babies have very different skull shapes. Here I am drawing a very round skull that is at the same time is slightly longer than the construction circle.

The neck is very short and thick. The shoulders start quite close to the head.

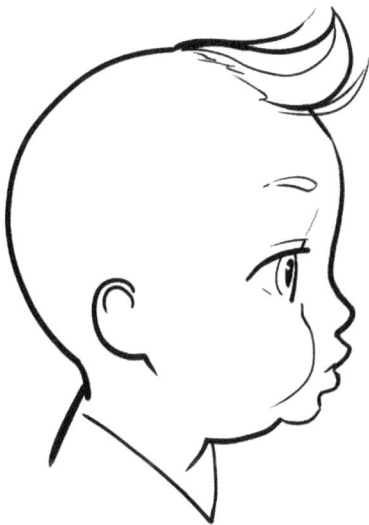

The cheek line from the side is very thinly drawn. It starts below the eye and runs almost parallel to the nose/mouth/chin area. The cheek line lies inside the face and does not connect with any other line.

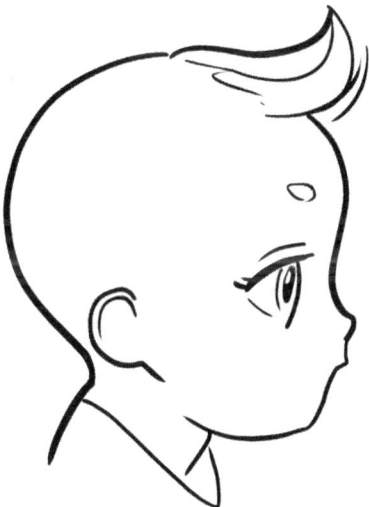

If you don't succeed in drawing the cheek and the mouth at first go, simplify this area by drawing only the upper lip.

You can now draw in the remaining area up to the chin as a whole, rounded shape. I made the eye a little larger here to give the baby a stronger manga look.

11.6 BABY FROM A ¾ VIEW

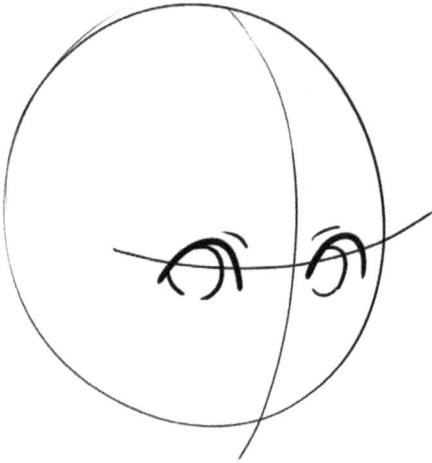

If you have practiced the front and side view sufficiently, then the 3/4 perspective will be easier for you.

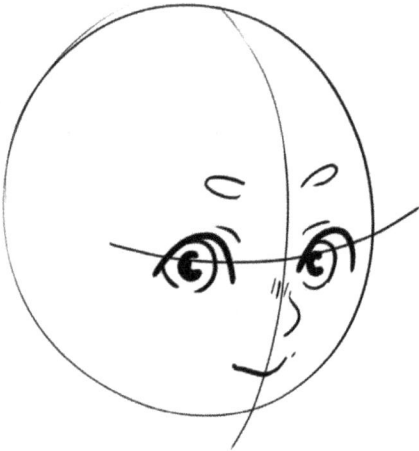

The difference to a chibi character are also here the protruding cheeks and the small chin in between.

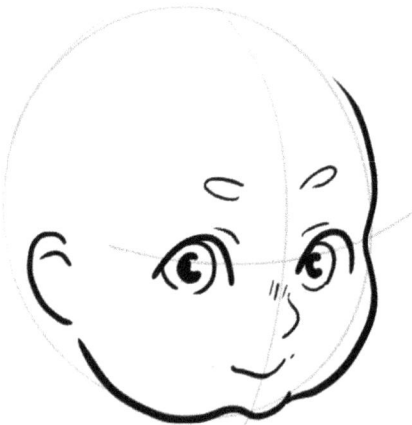

Have you noticed? I'm intentionally adding fewer and fewer measurement and construction lines.You are now so advanced that you can approach drawing faces more freely. Still feel free to measure from my drawing if needed, but feel free to rely more and more on your eye and accumulated knowledge.

This baby looks a little older because of the full head of hair. Some of the hair stands out and is curly and playful.

What I noticed is that it doesn't necessarily look strange on babies when the pupils float freely. It simply suits babies to have their eyes wide open and to try to see everything exactly with their intense gaze.

The neck is not visible here. The shoulders are already a bit broader, indicating a slightly older baby or even a toddler.

To emphasize the rosy cheeks, you can draw circles on the cheeks. Make sure that the lines are very thin and the circles are not complete, but slightly open. The back circle is very compressed due to the perspective.Individual hairs sticking out give the hairstyle more realism.

The drawing of a bright child is finished!

11.7 AGING PROCESS: FROM BABY TO GRANDPA

Depicting the complete aging process of a character is a super exercise to improve your drawing skills. First of all, try to draw my character and reading my notes. Drawings often look "easy", but as soon as you take pen and paper in your own hand, it doesn't work out so easily. This is normal and also one of the reasons why I describe the drawing steps in this book in such detail.

The text should help you to better understand what exactly I pay attention to when drawing. If the tracing of my character works well, try the same with your own character. The most important ages are: baby, teenager, young man, adult and old man.

BABY

The aging process of this character begins with him as a baby. The cheeks are large, the eyes are far down the face. The forehead is large and the hair is curly. The neck is barely visible. More detailed instructions on how to draw this baby can be found on the previous pages.

TEENAGER

The eyes are still quite large, but now more angular. The eyebrows are more pronounced. The hair is thicker and longer. The nose has also grown a bit longer, but still has a cute snub nose shape. The neck is more pronounced, but not too muscular yet. The forehead area is smaller than in the baby. The jawline still shows soft shapes, but the chubby cheeks are gone.

YOUNG MAN

You can find detailed step-by-step instructions for this character in the section "More adult characters step-by-step" (chapter 6.1).

Jaw and chin have completely formed. The eyes now appear smaller because the nose and especially the jaw area have grown. The neck is more muscular, the larynx is clearly visible. The forehead is no longer dominant because the lower part of the face is now significantly larger in comparison.

MAN AROUND 40

The standard procedure for drawing the first signs of aging is to start with forehead wrinkles, wrinkles around the eyes and nasolabial folds. You can see this approach to aging characters very often in anime.

At the same time, the character still retains a certain youthfulness at this age. Although this man has the first wrinkles, his eyes and other facial structures still look young.

In the next steps, simply adding wrinkles to the face will not be enough to make the character look believably older.

MAN AROUND 50

The tissue above the upper eyelid loses tension and increasingly overlaps the upper area of the eyes. Especially the outer eye areas are covered. The upper line of the eye merges with the wrinkles on the sides of the eye. This makes the person look a lot older. The lips fade with age, so I removed the line for the lower lip to make the mouth look older. Everything looks more fitting now, but the aging process still goes on...

MAN AROUND 60

Now we have to deal with the jaw line and the neck. Things are happening there, too. The tissue between the cheek and neck becomes "looser" and the jawline fades. I also draw the neck thinner and the previously clear line of the head-nicker muscle more wobbly. An uneven and thinner neck shows weakness and thus also indicates older age.

The tip of the chin remains clearly visible. It is surrounded by little tissue from the start. I draw in a slight hollow because it is appropriate. Basically, the more furrows and wrinkles we draw in, the older the person looks.

MAN AROUND 70

Now we can confidently add as many folds as we like. The only important thing is that we draw them in with a thin line and only in the places where wrinkles can actually appear.

On the forehead, for example, there can really be a lot of wrinkles - depending on how a person has "used" their forehead in their life. More wrinkles can also be added around the eyes. Especially under the eyes, many wrinkles can appear. In the mouth area, on the other hand, wrinkles are less common, but I think it still looks very cool in the manga to draw in a lot of wrinkles there.

MAN AROUND 80

In this example, we have not taken care of the hair at all. But of course a lot happens here with age. The eyebrows usually become scarce until they are hardly visible. Or the complete opposite happens and they grow out completely. For this reason, I've drawn the eyebrows here more playful on the one hand, while they get a little shorter on the outside.

The hair I draw a little more shaggy and playful. They are now only on the side and the back of the head.

Now that we are confident in drawing faces and heads, we can confidently approach drawing various head coverings.

Helmets, caps, and hats are largely extensions of the head. The head form or hairstyle often changes the design of the head cover – not the other way around.

Again, use lots of references, do your research and draw preliminary sketches. This will make your own designs believable and fun.

CHAPTER 12

HEADDRESSES UND NECK ACCESSORIES

12.1 HEADPHONES

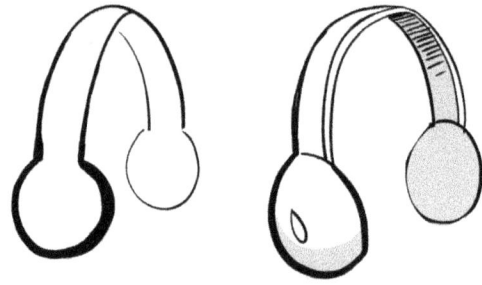

As a preliminary exercise, draw the headphones floating freely. This will make your final drawing on the character more accurate.

When drawing headphones, I like to start with the ear pad. Note that while this shape would be circular from the front, it appears compressed as an ellipse from this 3/4 view.

The headband of the headphones rounds around the head. It is often adjustable in length, so I'll draw in some shapes to illustrate this.

Again, it's important to pick out a few references. You can also trace a photo template in its entirety. Or you can create your very own design from several references. However, this requires intensive research to make your own headphones feel real.

(3)

The headphones need some distance from the head, so I draw a shadow under the headband. This shadow has a wavy shape to show that it falls on hair and the hair is uneven.

(4)

Notice the different thickness of the lines on the headphones. The inner parts and design elements have thin lines, while the outer lines and the lines that have a shadow are quite thick.

The ear pad is round, so the shadow has a gradient. The side of the headband is completely in the shadow. Since the cables are further away from the body, the shadow is naturally further away from the object.

(5)

12.2 MAGICIAN HAT

Drawing a manga girl as a magician is always a very popular task with my students.

However, what happens to many is that they draw the bottom of the hat too small. If you trace the distance from her neck to the top of the hat with your fingers, it will be about the same as the width of the overhanging lower part of the hat. Draw this too wide rather than too narrow.

Draw the seams and folds of the hat with thin, interrupted lines. Especially in the upper part, where the top of the hat rolls up, there are creases in the fabric.

The bow on the hat in this case is in the shape of a butterfly. Instead of the bow, of course, you can use completely different shapes.

The magic necklace has a similar shape to the top of the hat. Similar shapes within a drawing make character designs look more coherent.

We further extend the character's curling design by also drawing the hair a bit more sticking out and twisted. The longer hairstyle fits the character well.

The protruding hair expresses the joy of experimentation and an urge for independence. These qualities are perfect for a self-confident magician.

A wide collar indicates that she wears a coat. I draw magical ornaments with a thin line along the outlines.

Now we have already drawn quite a lot. To keep the picture organized, I give everything its own base color. This way we can quickly see the difference between the hair and the hat. The differences in brightness also indicate that there are different materials and colors.

The most important shadow in this image is the one below the hat. This runs once around her head to show that the hat curves inward. Also note the curve of the drop shadow on the top of the head. This shadow edge once again indicates that the head is very round.

I draw other shadows under the chin, under the hair, under the upper eyelid, and the hair behind the neck.

To give the hat more three-dimensionality, we shade the entire right side of the top of the hat. At the top of the hat, where it curls in, we can use quite a bit of darkness.

Note that although the bow is mostly on the shaded side, it still gets some light from the protruding shapes. You can also achieve more depth by adding a shadow between the neck and the collar.

7

Finally, I work out the eyes. In addition, a slightly darker shadow is added behind the collar on the hair. The bow I also give places with more darkness. A few light spots on the hat and the bow also give these shapes more three-dimensionality. But be careful not to make these light spots too bright. Otherwise it will quickly look like the surface is made of metal.

In the end, let your creativity run wild and draw her magical animal companions or other accessories.

12.3 VIKING

As a basis for this Viking I use a character we developed in one of the previous chapters. Therefore, for the head construction, take a look at the instructions in the chapter "Other head shapes". This example will focus on drawing the helmet.

①

②

We'll start with the rectangular head shape (without a circle), which gets wider towards the bottom. Note that the area between the nose and chin is the largest and widest part of this character's face. The forehead, on the other hand, is very small. The preliminary drawing of our angular head shape serves us perfectly as a guide.

Both the beard and the eyebrows have this bulky character. When drawing these elements, make sure that the beard hairs differ in direction and size - like an area of grass. Sometimes they have thin lines, sometimes thicker.

The upper hairs are tied back. The hair strands start at the hairline and run roundly to the back. The upper eyelid is not visible at all, because it is hidden by the low-set eyebrows.

3

Now you can add forehead wrinkles and the wrinkles under the eyes with thin lines. The lower lip is only very slightly indicated, while the upper lip is also covered by the beard.

The armor rests on the shoulders and is thus placed quite high up. However, the character does not have a particularly long neck either.

4

There are also protective flaps on the sides. They are movable and are designed to protect the face from side blows.

Make sure that the head and ears must fit under the helmet.

Draw the belt buckle with special care. Sometimes such small elements enhance a drawing immensely.

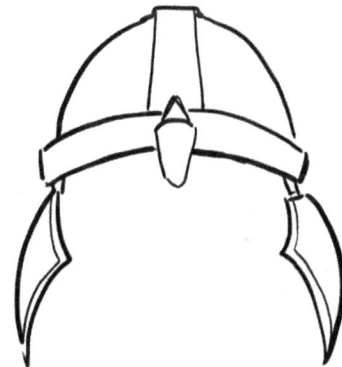

The helmet basically has the shape of a cap. The lines are much stiffer and firmer compared to cloth headgear. There is also a nose bone guard in the front center.

5

Next, we add extended protection for the nose and cheeks. Also, the helmet gets more parts on the forehead. These look almost like eyebrows and give the character more fierceness.

6

The helmet is made of iron. You can show this by drawing small dots around the edges. In addition, you can draw another thin border line for some shapes.

7

I added two impressive horns to the helmet to show that this is no ordinary warrior. He seems to enjoy a higher status.

Now I give the helmet and the armor their own shades of grey. This makes the drawing more structured and easier to "read". You can add some black shadows under the helmet and under the shoulder armor.

Now comes a layer of shadow to give the objects more shape. The eyes can be completely in shadow. There is shadow on the underside of the horns, as well as under the nose guard, the lower side of the beard, under the shoulder guards and under the belt. To give the helmet more roundness, shadow also runs along the outer line.

8

9

I couldn't resist the urge to add another sword pommel. XD I love drawing armor and swordsmen! Whereas he's probably more likely to carry an axe on his back. After all, he is a Viking. Also notice that I gave his eyes little dots of light to finish off. This brings more liveliness to his look.

12.4 TOP HAT

The top hat has a cylindrical shape. However, do not draw it too stiff and straight. All its lines are curved. On the sides, the lines are slightly bent inward. The top line, on the other hand, is also curved upward.

Even though the likelihood of a top hat appearing in your manga story might be low, drawing this particular hat is a great exercise.

You can go a little deeper into the subject of shading in particular. You should start with the lines around the head - where the cylinder begins. Note that this headgear also has some distance to the head and the line sticks out slightly.

The head shape can now be erased and the top hat is given a basic shading. Note that we see the top hat slightly from below. Therefore, lines that bend around the top hat are curved upwards.

You can draw the first shadows on the sides of the upper cylinder area and on the underside of the brim. For further shading, however, the upper part of the hat will be the most interesting.

6

Since the top of the hat is round, we need to draw in a shading gradient. I do this by getting lighter and lighter with my hatching towards the light stripe.

7

A tip for advanced users: Put some light in the shadow area. Look closely. On the left side, there is now a strip that is really only very slightly lighter.

8

The white stripe gets a similar shading as the dark body of the top hat. But the shading is lighter in comparison, because the base is lighter. A shadow on a white surface looks lighter than a shadow on a dark background.

9

10

Now you can create even more three-dimensionality by adding a rather bright stripe in the light area of the top hat.

Note, however, that this light stripe is not white, but a light gray. If you were to make the stripe white, it would merge with the background and the top hat would not stand out as much from the background.

The shadow under the hat rounds around the head.

12.5 BASEBALL CAP

For the cap, I like to start with the front part, the visor. Here, too, it's a good idea to completely sketch out the face first. You can then place the cap over it afterwards.

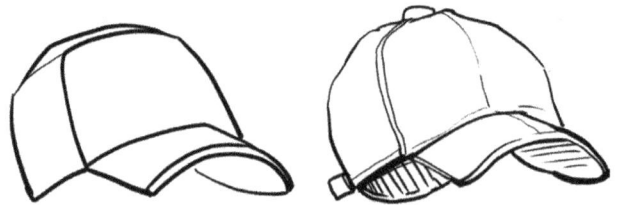

The front area of the cap is a little tricky. Make sure that this sunshade has a certain thickness and the lines are all curved.

With the outlines we determine not only the size, but also the fabric from which the cap is made.

If you draw the whole cap with rather straight, stiff lines, it will look like a harder fabric. If, on the other hand, you draw the outlines wavier, with varying line thickness, the cap will look less sturdy.

So the material looks like a softer fabric. Once I've indicated the cap, I draw in the figure's hair, which is still sticking out of the back of the headgear. This completes the outline and you can take care of the inner design of the cap.

First, I draw in the seams of the cap with thin lines. This makes the cap look much more realistic.

The next step is to put a logo on the front of the cap. Here, of course, you can be creative.

Do not draw the shading under the sunshade of the canopy too small. The shade stands out quite far and casts a large shadow. The lower edge of the shadow follows the anatomy of the face.

The nose stands out, so the shadow makes an upward curve at the nose.

More shadows are added under the ear, under the chin, under the nose and under the lower lip. This credibly defines the light-shadow situation.

12.6 SPACE HELMET

For the space helmet, I use the chibi character from the front view.

Again, I recommend that you do the extra work of first pre-drawing the character complete with hair. Then you can place the helmet "on top". If you were to start with the helmet right away and then fill in the cutouts with the face, you would have much more difficulty drawing the correct proportions.

The basic outlines of the helmet are slightly thicker, while the internal components and patterns have quite thin lines.

If you want to add more screws and components, look for pictures of machine components on the Internet and have fun trying them out.

We want to draw a believable cosmonaut helmet. We don't need a scientific degree for this, but a little research and a few thoughts should go a long way.

The helmet has rivets or screws. This gives the impression that the helmet is also held together somehow and is made of several components.

Small headlights on top of the sides and a hose with a connection to the oxygen tank give the drawing more credibility. The helmet seems to be really functional.

Our eyes like symmetry. That's why I try not to overload either side of the helmet with technology. Much is the same on both sides, but there are still slight variations.

The air tube on the right, leading away from the helmet towards the back, is a larger shape. The drawing "tilts" to the right as a result. To compensate, I therefore draw an antenna on the left side. I also added the buttons to the lower left of the face. This makes the image more visually balanced.

It's not a bad idea at all to practice shading on such technical equipment as this helmet. This is usually somewhat easier than on a face. The shadow-light relationships are simply much more complex on a human face.

My light source here is at the top. This automatically means that the lower sides of all components of the helmet can be colored darker.

I'll use only one darkness level for now. For round objects we would actually need a shadow gradient. However, since we are drawing simplified, a flat shadow is quite sufficient.

6

Note that I also placed a shadow along the top and sides of the helmet, each along the rearmost line. This gives the entire helmet more roundness. The screw heads are also slightly in the shadow, making them objects that stick out from the helmet.

I color the visor of the helmet with a darker shade of darkness. This looks super flat at first glance. But don't worry: there are still some steps to come.

A tip at this point for digital artists: Set the layer of the visor to "Multiply". That way you can still see the lines of your character.

7

In the next step we set the shading of the character. There is a distance between the inside of the helmet and the head of the chibi boy. To visually represent this distance, we need a shadow that the helmet casts on the character. The size of the shadow on the character defines how much space the head has inside the helmet.

The hair also has some distance to the face, so there are shadows under it as well. Under the upper eyelids we also put some shadow. Already the drawing looks much more three-dimensional.

Finally, we add glossy effects to the visor.

Digitally, it's easy: I draw white stripes over the visor on a new layer and lower the opacity of the layer. This gives me semi-transparent stripes.

Traditional artists can resort to a white gel pen for a similar effect or, for example, use a kneaded eraser to lightly erase the appropriate areas.

I also color some objects, such as the hoses, darker. This emphasizes that the helmet and the hoses are made of different materials. This gives our drawing the final look.

Finally, I'd like to share with you my process in creating the manga character on the cover of this book. It originally took me about two days to complete the drawing. After that, when I recorded the drawing process on video for my online course, it took "only" four hours. When you know exactly what you're drawing, it just goes faster.

In this book I can only show you a few steps. But I hope it still brings inspiration and some interesting insights into my drawing process.

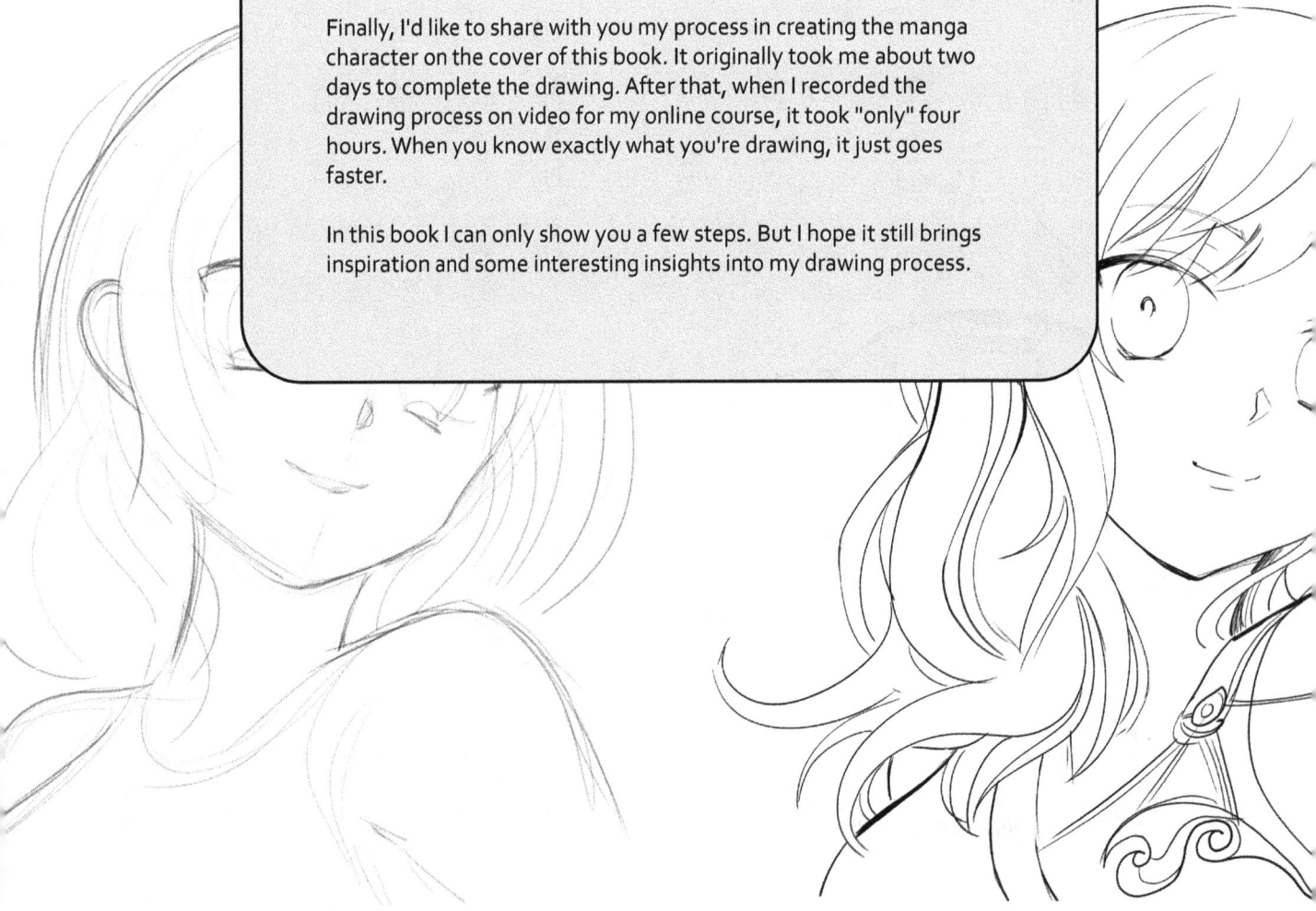

CHAPTER 13

COVER DRAWING STEP BY STEP

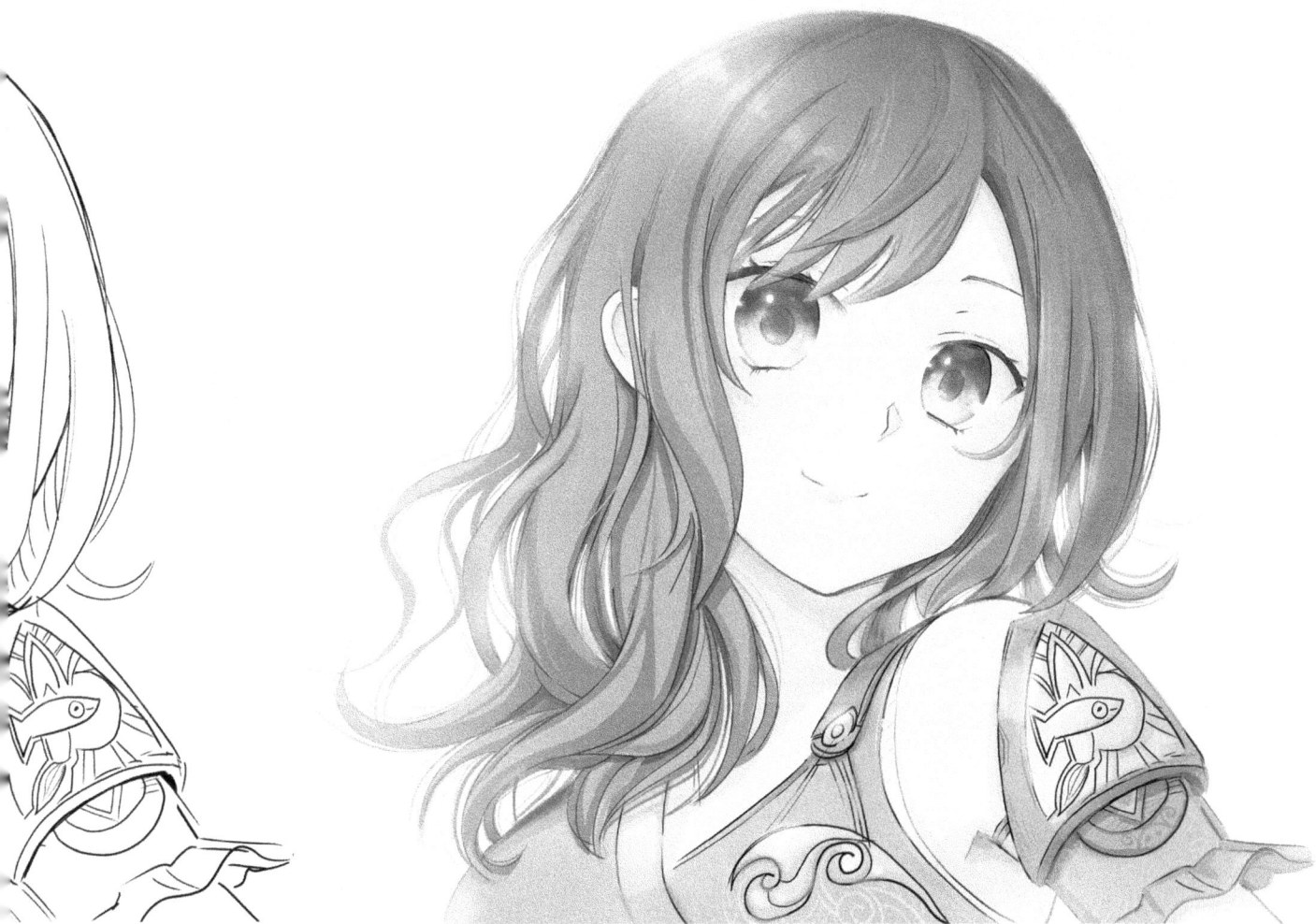

13 COVER DRAWING

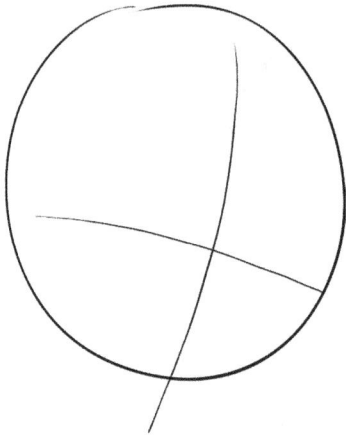

①

We start in the classic way with a circle and the crossing of the eye line and the center line of the face. This way we define the direction of the gaze and the perspective at the same time.

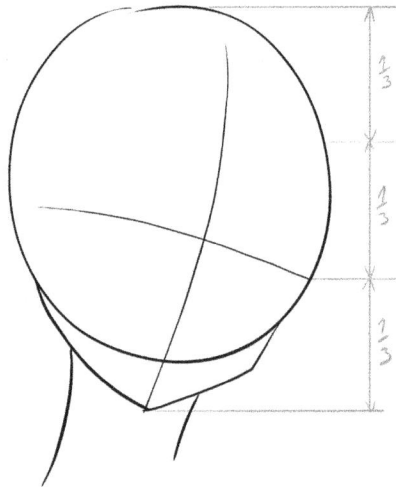

②

The second step is to add the chin-jaw line. Make sure that there is only a little chin and that the eye line is quite far down in the face. After all, it is supposed to be a cute character. We achieve this characteristic by having little chin and a lot of forehead.

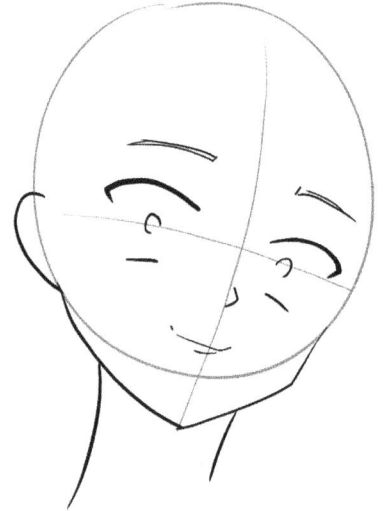

③

In the third step, I sketch in the face and ears. This is only for orientation at first. I work out the facial features later. But it's important to draw everything roughly first to see how the elements fit together best. The elaborations begin only when the correct positions and proportions have been found.

But we are still in the draft stage. Therefore, light sketching is sufficient.

Let's continue with the upper part of the body. The approximate shapes of this motif are already sketched.

At this point, it is still relatively easy to make major changes. For example, if the head and the body do not fit together, the body needs to be made larger, or the angle of the tilted head needs to be adjusted, you still have the opportunity to do this now. At this stage of the drawing it is important to find the right dynamics of the figure before we go into the details.

Now I will come to the hair. These take a very central role in this motif. They should support and strengthen the dynamics of the body.

This time I don't start with individual lines or strands, but draw a rough silhouette. This allows me to see quickly whether the overall shape fits or not.

If hair, head and body fit well together, you can continue with the final drawing.

Orient yourself to the sketched hair silhouette and draw in individual strands. I always start with the largest strands and then divide them further and further. The very thin strands of hair come only at the end.

The hair silhouette serves as our orientation (as described above). With the outlines, the hair shape is further clarified.

In this step, I also drew the face more cleanly so that the hair and face fit together nicely. I had to do a lot of trial and error here! So it's quite normal that you don't immediately find the right proportions.

6

Now let's move on to the clothing. I wanted to give this figure a cool fantasy look. Therefore, I chose clothing that reminds of a light, magical armor. For once, I got by without doing much research here and just added a few buckles and embellishments as I felt.

Not everything always has to "make sense". Sometimes it's enough if it just looks good.

7

In this case, I put a lot of effort into the eyes. I have actually never drawn so many highlights in the eyes.

The eyes are often the point on which one focuses first as a viewer. People often look each other in the eye first. For this reason, it is especially important that the look fits. From this perspective, it was not at all easy to direct the gaze of the figure so that it really looks at you.

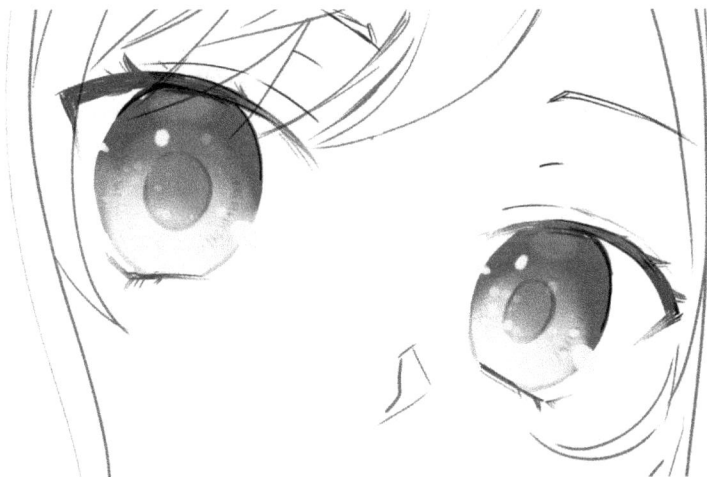

The left and right eyes have quite large differences in shape and angle of view.

Notice how round the pupil is in the left eye. Compare it with the right eye, where it is squeezed and oval.

Also, the left pupil is more tilted to the left, while the back pupil is tilted to the right.

Here I really had to try out a lot until I found the right positions.

9

Satisfied (and exhausted) from drawing the eyes, I set to work on the base darks of the hair. Coloring the basic colors or darks of the hair, skin and clothes is totally relaxing for me. It allows me to catch my breath and prepare for the next, more challenging steps.

10

For the colors I had previously looked for well-matching colors. Either from other drawings or photos or generated color harmonies.

So I no longer have to worry about which colors to use, instead I can concentrate on distributing the colors properly.

11

Now gradients and first shadows come into play.

Especially the gradient in the hair is important. It starts dark at the top and becomes lighter towards the bottom. This creates a high degree of threedimensionality.

Round shapes are generally represented threedimensionally by gradients. The head, the arm and the torso are such round shapes, which I can quickly make more impressive with simple gradients.

I draw drop shadows under the head, under the hair and under the individual pieces of clothing.

12

Next, I work out the hair.

The light comes from slightly above on the left. Everything that turns away from this light source becomes darker. So I darken the right and the lower sides of the hair strands.

13

Finally, I add light effects. Digitally, this works quite easily. Compared to the previous step, it looks like I changed a lot. Only a few light gradients have been added. But these can have a great effect. I use a soft brush in white and set the layer function to "copy into each other" or "soft light". Alter-natively, I simply brush in gradients with white and lower the opacity of these gradients. When drawing with pencil and ink, you can also you can build up light situations. However, it is a bit more difficult. For beginners, it's easier to practice digitally because you can try out so much. Then, once you've developed a good feel for light and shadow, you can also super con-fidently create masterpieces using traditional drawing methods!

I like to keep switching back and forth between digital and traditional drawing methods. I also enjoy drawing both imaginative manga and realistic portraits.

This variety has helped me a lot in keeping my drawing fun. At the same time, it has made me a more flexible artist. All methods and styles have their benefits and drawbacks. That's why it's important to learn things from a wide variety of art fields. Of course, only as long as you feel like it and enjoy it.

LEARNING IS DEFINITELY DIFFICULT WITHOUT FUN! :D

MAXIMKO
ART

IMPRINT

Copyright @Maxim Simonenko
Koßfelderstraße 7 II 18055 Rostock

ISBN: 978-3-910312-09-8

Editor:Thomas Zimmer
Translation: Aline Zimmer // Layout: Andrea Köster

Cover design: Sprudelkopf Design – Jasmin Raif, www.sprudelkoepfe.com
Cover art elements: iStockphoto, ©PaulMaguire, ©Punnarong, ©Kurtikam

Illustrations: Maxim Simonenko, www.maximko.de